THE
5
PERCENTER

DEFYING DEATH AND EMBRACING LIFE

THE
5
PERCENTER

DEFYING DEATH AND EMBRACING LIFE

HOW STRENGTH, LOVE AND GOLF
DROVE A REMARKABLE RECOVERY

MICHAEL MURPHY

LZ

Published by Learning Zone Books, an imprint of Brisance Books Group LLC
The publisher is not responsible for websites or their content that are not owned by the publisher.

Learning Zone LLC
3219 E. Camelback Road #355
Phoenix, AZ 85018
602-315-9700

Printed in the United States of America
First Edition: June 2018

ISBN: 978-1-944194-50-5

Back cover photo credit: Michael Brady

062018

PRAISE FOR.... *THE 5 PERCENTER*

Mike's story is truly inspiring and shows how a positive attitude, a strong will to live and the presence of a loving family can make a difference beyond what even the best medical care can accomplish.

— David J. Engel, MD
NY Presbyterian Hospital Columbia University Medical Center

When I heard about Murph's injury I immediately jumped on a plane to NY and NY Presbyterian Hospital. We were very close friends in Law School and remain close now. When I saw him lying unconscious with wires coming out of every part of his body I was truly bereft, it was as though the oxygen had left my body. Only recently I was laughing with him at dinner in LA with my godson Riley. He was looking great in a new suit and tie and 25 pounds lighter. We were all so incredibly happy. Now, it's great to have him back and I can't wait for the next chapter in his recovery.

— Bill Macdonald, Law School friend and Hollywood producer

The story of Mike Murphy's sudden heart attack, coma, impairment and recovery illustrates how each of us walks a thin line, often without appreciating our good fortune in being healthy. The lessons from Mike's ordeal will be useful to every reader. I am very happy that we still get to see each other and still get to laugh together.

— Cort Delany, Law School friend

I was with my brother in the hospital when he couldn't breathe on his own, couldn't speak and couldn't walk. Now we can play golf together and he's written this book. It's truly amazing and wonderful. I love that we talk several times a week and I'm very proud of his always positive attitude and his passion for life.

— Tim Murphy, brother

As a seasoned nurse practitioner, I can say that Michael's recovery is remarkable. As his sister in-law, I can say that I am beyond grateful for his recovery. Michael is a beloved member of our family and we always have a great time when we get together for family fun.

— Paula Pillone, sister-in-law

Michael Murphy has overcome some significant challenges in his lifetime but none more life threatening than his cardiac arrest. Through it all his courage and determination served him well. With the help and support of his family and close friends Michael persevered and has not only defied the odds but surpassed expectations. His sunny Irish personality belies the struggle he waged to arrive at his current situation and he is working toward new goals every day. I look forward to seeing the next chapter, Michael!

— Barbara Pillone, mother-in-law

I was at the hospital when my dad was still unconscious, then he spoke and then walked after a nurse said he wouldn't. Today we can play golf together, that's amazing. I've always gone to him when I needed advice or help and he's always been there for me and I will always be there for him. I love my dad. He has always been my biggest supporter and I'm so proud of him for writing this book.

— Riley Murphy, son

I was with my Dad when he woke up in NY Presbyterian Hospital and he smiled at me. I knew then that he would recover. I was there to help him dress for his first adventure out of the hospital. His amazing journey has reaffirmed my decision to become a doctor, which I love. And I love being able to be with my Dad, to laugh with him and speak with him often.

— Ian Murphy, son

The Five Percenter *is a dramatic and life-affirming story about a man who literally returned from the dead. Mike Murphy's miraculous recovery from a massive heart attack and traumatic brain injury is both amazing and inspiring.*

— Scott Garley, Law School classmate and friend

Relearning to play golf gave Mike a path to mental and physical recovery. From his wheelchair six years ago, to now shooting in the low 80s and walking all his rounds, is a miracle. Congrats, Mike. Job well done!

— Kerry Graham, LPGA Hall of Fame, Mike's Golf Instructor

FOREWORD

From when I first met Michael, I was impressed by his intelligence, his kindness and generosity, his positive attitude, and his loyalty and dedication to friends and family. A strong work ethic and drive to 'close the deal' seemed to come naturally to him. Michael has been described as a bulldog as well as a creative genius depending on what the situation required. Most who know Michael are familiar with his mischievous side which is part of his charm and one reason he is so much fun to be around. Michael has always had a true love and passion for life, both work and fun, which is why it was such a shock when he came so close to leaving it so early.

I have experienced two moments of all-encompassing shock and heartache in my life. First when I was nine, when my father had a heart attack while reeling in a Marlin off Montauk Point. The second, when I received that phone call from paramedics in the Delta Sky Lounge telling me that Michael had collapsed. It is incredible, in such moments, how the world suddenly narrows to a singular focus of trying to keep the one you love. Tragically, we lost my father that day but Michael found a way to pull through. I am eternally grateful to Nurse Ray, to the doctors at Jamaica Hospital who immediately applied hypothermia, to all of the doctors at Columbia and NYU. We had to make tough decisions along the way and my and Michael's family were all there to support us. To them as well, I am eternally grateful.

Spending a total of three months with Michael in critical care, acute rehabilitation, and sub-acute rehabilitation hospitals—and experiencing his return to life—was unforgettable. There were comical moments like trying to explain to Michael that he wasn't in a hotel, there was no hotel bar and there was no chance of being moved to a room with a king-sized bed. There were enlightening moments like explaining to Michael how a clock face works and having to agree with him that it was complicated. There were gut-wrenching but inspiring moments like watching Michael being escorted down the hall with a therapist on each side, being held aloft by a harness-on-wheels contraption and seeing him wave to the nurses, doctors and others in the hallway as if he had just arrived at the golf club. One of the nurses told me that Michael's 'ace in the hole' is his positive attitude and tenacity. Those characteristics have defined Michael over his entire life and they, in addition to great medical care, are why he is with us today.

I remember the first plane trip that Michael and I took about six months after his incident. It was the first time that we would be spending more than a day off the island of Manhattan. On the cab ride to the airport, staring at the grey steel of the Queensborough bridge blending into a dawning New York skyline, I thought back to the marathon of hospitals and therapy… and managing Michael's care and work and moving. I had a strange and wonderful sense of satisfaction, that we had made it through the hardest part. Michael was still here, he had found a way to stay on this earth with me and though our lives would never be the same, our love for each other was intact—it had pulled us through and, like Michael, would only become stronger.

Pamela Murphy

PROLOGUE

It's the afternoon of October 7, 2011 and I am on the ground in the Delta Lounge in JFK Airport. I am dead. I have just come from a meeting at Trump Tower in NYC with Eric Trump and a few executives where my company, Boutique Club, is working on a deal to help market the Trump Residences in Puerto Rico. I am scheduled to fly to Las Vegas to meet with my wonderful wife, Pam, to celebrate my 54th birthday. We are living in New York City and Pam had gone to Las Vegas earlier in the week for a conference.

The meeting goes a little long and, as usual, I am already running late for my flight. Traffic to the airport is ridiculous, as always in NYC, and I email my long-time friend and partner, Jay Di Giulio, that I am likely to miss my flight. I leave my taxi at a full run. I get to the gate where the door is closing in front of me. Despite my pleas, the flight attendant doesn't relent and closes the door. I am not happy.

I run to the Delta lounge to try to book a new flight. When I arrive at the lounge, I collapse, unconscious, right in front of the reception desk. I guess the good Lord didn't want me up in Heaven, just yet, telling Him how to run the place… and the Devil just didn't want me at all. Then a woman appears behind me on her way out of the lounge to catch a flight to Paris. This was Ray, a Johns Hopkins-trained Registered Nurse, who—to this day—I thank for saving my life. She immediately provides CPR, though I remained unconscious. At the time no one working in the lounge could locate a defibrillator. I am rushed to Jamaica Hospital Medical Center in Queens, where there is now, ironically, a Trump Pavilion. Thankfully, Jamaica Hospital was in the practice of applying hypothermia in my type of case and they were able to preserve what was left of my brain. I am diagnosed with cardiac arrest and a traumatic anoxic brain injury (TBI), which is interesting because a lot of my friends would say that I already had a brain injury. It just wasn't all that traumatic for them.

CHAPTER 1

It's April 8TH of 2012 and I am heading to Mass with my wife, Pam. She's an incredible woman—as wonderful and loving as she is beautiful. It is Easter Sunday and I have not been to Mass for several years, despite my clear need for contrition. It's a noon Mass at Most Holy Trinity Catholic Church in Mamaroneck, New York. This is the Church that I grew up in and spent a lot of time in as a young child. As a matter of fact, I used to go to Mass every day and was an altar boy at Holy Trinity through 6TH grade. Early in my young life, I even had thoughts of being a priest until Father John told me, without hesitation, that was unlikely. The Catholic Church dodged a bullet there. Even after my injury, even though my memory has been badly impaired, I can still say many Catholic prayers by rote. Pam is also Catholic and is more devout and spiritual than me, so we now attend Mass once a month (a compromise). Most Holy Trinity Church is small but beautiful, with brilliant stained-glass windows and sculptures of St. Joseph, St. John the Baptist, and the Virgin Mary. A large sculpture of Jesus on the cross graces the back of the Church and can be seen by all the parishioners. The Church still has organ music and a full choir singing uplifting hymns. The priest was much more casual than I recalled, and I didn't remember that he spoke with a microphone the last time I was here; that's how long it had been. He gave his homily from a raised platform and the theme was "being a better person." I have thought about that a lot since that Sunday, and, while I think that I've always been a pretty good person, I have never given a lot to charity or worked with homeless or destitute people. I'm hoping that I have the opportunity to work again. I have not worked or had any income since my TBI. I figure that the good Lord kept me alive for a reason and I would like to find a way to give something back to Him and to my friends and family. I always start my day, after kissing Pam and telling her that I love her, with a short prayer to thank the Lord for being alive and for keeping me and my family safe, healthy, and happy.

My memory has essentially left me since my TBI and it used to be one of my strongest assets and something I was most proud of. The memories I do have are mostly positive, as is my attitude towards life right now. This book is my therapy and writing it has been a very interesting and wonderful journey for me. I am so happy to be alive that nothing else really matters, except for those closest to me. There are not words to adequately convey my gratitude and love for the amazing and generous people that I'm lucky enough to call family, extended family and close friends. It's my hope that this book gives the other 5 Percenters—those few and fortunate who beat the odds and survive—affirmation and inspiration that life, though difficult at times after an injury like ours, is still a wonderful gift that should be embraced with passion. This is not the end of good things, but, in a real sense, a new beginning. The book is called *The 5 Percenter* because only five percent of people who have had cardiac arrest with a lack of oxygen for as long as I did survive at all. I know that I am a very lucky man and plan to try to make every day magical.

CHAPTER 2

My Father, Timothy Francis Murphy and my Mother, Mary Patricia Higgins, were born in Blackrock, County Cork, Ireland. I believe that my father was a blacksmith or carpenter. They were like many other couples in Ireland, poor and looking for something better. I'll never know specifically why they left Ireland or how they found the money to do it, but in 1955 Tim and Mary Pat got on the Queen Mary ocean liner to a new life in the United States and New York. I think they thought that they could not have children and that the United States would provide new opportunities for them. They settled in the town of Mamaroneck in Westchester County, New York (one of the most affluent counties in the country) and rented a small apartment there. I think that my father first worked as a part-time carpenter and janitor for NY Telephone Company.

I was born on October 1, 1956, foiling all their plans for independence, and my brother, Tim, came along three years later, on March 1, 1960. As I recall, my Father also became the Superintendent for our apartment building. I do still remember the heat from the boiler room in the basement of our building. My father would take me down there to make sure I knew to stay away from that part of the building. In a few years my father was a supervisor at that same NY Telephone Company office that was within walking distance from our apartment.

In Mamaroneck my Mother was very homesick for the country that had been home to her for more than 30 years and she and I went back to Ireland to see her family and friends in 1959. During that trip my Mother decided that she wanted to stay in Ireland. When she told my Father that she wanted to stay, my Father told her that she could stay but that she had to send me back because I was an American citizen. He was a tough, stubborn Irishman. Thankfully, we both came back. We went to Ireland as a complete family in 1964. It was to be my Father's last visit to his homeland after leaving it for the United States. I believe my Father wanted us to visit Ireland with him at least once, so his parents and my Mother's parents could see their grandchildren. This was very important to them. It must have been incredibly hard for my Father to cobble together the funds for the trip. We traveled by boat on The Queen Mary, which must have been a lot of fun for my parents with two impish and restless young boys, aged seven and four. To this day, that is the only cruise liner I have ever traveled on. I don't remember anything about the trip except that I know that we went to Blarney Castle on March 28, 1964 so that I could kiss the Blarney Stone. Blarney Castle is only about five miles from Cork, where both my parents were born and where they lived for many years. Kissing the Blarney Stone is supposed to give one the "gift of gab," eloquence and skill at flattery. It was pouring rain on the day I kissed the Stone, typical weather in Ireland, and I was covered in paper to protect me. I had to get on the ground and lean back into a large hole in the ground. I was kissing everything I could until finally a man pulled me out and said, "You did it lad, congratulations." I guess it must have worked because I've always been full of it.

My parents wanted to make sure that my brother and I had the best education possible, so we enrolled at Most Holy Trinity School in Mamaroneck. The nice thing was that it was walking distance from our house. My parents bought a house on Bradley Street in Mamaroneck that my brother still lives in now with his wife Siobhan. I was schooled by nuns from kindergarten through 6TH grade and went to Mass every day. As soon as I was old enough, I became an altar boy and got to wear cool robes and go backstage into the sacristy to help the priest prepare for and clean up after Mass. I was a very good student and received many academic awards. The nuns would give out silver and gold pins whenever a student got a grade of better than 90% in a class. I cherished those pins and wore them on my little blue blazer to Mass on Sundays. I would come home for lunch every day to watch *Jeopardy* on TV. I got pretty good at the game and still watch it now when I can. Sadly, I think I got more answers correct when I was nine than I can now.

Even though I wore a blue blazer and went to Mass, I was far from saintly. I was a precocious child and not afraid to speak my mind or yell at my parents. Even though I was a small kid, I thought that I was pretty tough. My father was a lot tougher, however, and he had a belt that he was not afraid to use to prove it. Tough love and corporal punishment was the way of the Irish (and many American parents in the 1960s) and I went to bed with a red rear-end many nights. I'm sure that I deserved whatever he delivered. My father never hit me with his hand or his fist, although he probably should have. Even though I would never fault my father for using a belt for disciplining me, I have never even thought of hitting my sons, Ian and Riley. I always preferred more subtle forms of punishment.

We lived very close to the Long Island Sound, so my parents made sure that my brother and I knew how to swim at a young age. I learned how to swim at a public beach called Harbor Island, which was very close to our house. My coach was Steve Johnson. Even then, he was a legend at Harbor Island and wore a Speedo every day at 40 years old and still looked good. I took to the water easily and was competing in swimming events for Harbor Island in 5TH and 6TH grades. My most vivid memory is the murky salt water. We swam competitively in the Long Island Sound with two large concrete posts, set 25 yards apart, and wires that made the lanes. I was very small, very competitive, and very fast. I learned how to do the butterfly stroke well and competed both in freestyle and butterfly events. In the summertime we would live on the beach and in the water; it was cheap fun.

In 6ᵀᴴ grade, I realized that my Mom was working, as well as my Father, because we joined a club called Orienta Beach Club in Mamaroneck. My Mother was a very accomplished seamstress and designed and created clothes for several very wealthy clients. Our dining room had two sewing machines and was always strewn with clothes waiting to be tailored. She worked from that dining room for several years. Eventually, she moved to a building owned by a friend who ran an antique store in Mamaroneck. She was so good that one of her wealthy clients financed her business for her. The store allowed her to have her own space; which provided some independence for her and a much better opportunity to expand her business. Many of her clients were wealthy men who were more comfortable going to a place of business than a home. I think that it was a little difficult for my Father at first to have a wife with a paying job. But it was very good for my Mother to be able to get out of the house and do what she did best in a more pleasant place. And the additional money was important and welcome.

My parents both wanted to ensure that my brother and I would have the best possible education. They came to America so that they could have the chance to be more successful than they could be in Ireland. Once Tim and I came along they also wanted us to have every possible opportunity for success. To that end, I left Holy Trinity School in 7ᵀᴴ grade and went to Iona Preparatory School, in New Rochelle. Iona was an all-boys, Catholic school run by the Christian Brothers. The Brothers were very serious about academics and equally serious about sports. I did very well in school and won a few academic awards. I also was a pitcher on the baseball team.

Despite my diminutive size (I was about 5'3 through 8TH grade) I was tough, scrappy, and a very good athlete. I loved baseball, liked the control of being a pitcher—and I was good at it. The first sport I learned how to play at home was hurling, which my Father had played in Ireland. It taught me how to have good eye-hand coordination and how to hit a ball, which helped a lot for baseball. We had two good seasons at Iona. I don't remember much about my time at Iona, but I do remember two of the Brothers. One was Italian, and he had very dark, black hair. He was very nice to me. I think he taught History and English. The other Brother was Irish, a huge man with red hair who called me (and everyone) "Herm." "Hey, Herm, what do you think you're doing?" or "Hey, Herm, get to class!" The Irish brother was very scary when he was meting out punishment because he was so big. We got 'shots' for bad behavior. Shots were basically smacks on the butt with a paddle. You could get shots for being late to class, for yelling in the hallways, or just being out of line in general. I heard "Two shots for you, Mr. Murphy" often. Because I was well trained in the art of corporal punishment, my cheeks were usually red already. Although I have never used any corporal punishment on my children I don't think my Father or the Brothers did anything wrong. In the 1960s it was a very typical and accepted method of discipline.

CHAPTER 3

I started swimming competitively in 5TH grade, and I was good. I won a lot of medals and trophies throughout my swimming career. When I was in 5TH and 6TH grades we were Westchester County YMCA Champions. I loved winning—and collecting the hardware. Both my Mother and Father got involved as timekeepers during my meets. Each lane had an adult with a stopwatch and my Mom got to know all my competitors well. One of those competitors was Tim Wallace. Tim was one of 10 children and I loved going to his house, which was always a mad house. He was a great swimmer and is a great guy. He also was very handsome and, with his looks and great personality, he attracted a lot of girls at parties. So, we spent a lot of time together during our summers in high school and college. During summers in high school we went to dance parties together every weekend at The Pandemonium at Larchmont Yacht Club and other clubs. We also both loved touch football and would play every weekend during the summer. Tim was the quarterback and I was his favorite wide receiver. We were both very competitive and won a lot more often than we lost. Tim and I stayed close through our college years and beyond and kept our gridiron tradition alive with a big touch football game during the Thanksgiving break. It was always great fun. Tim married Patsy Benziger around the same time I married my first wife. Patsy was, and is, very beautiful, spirited, and funny. We had a great time together when Tim and I were roommates in New York City. Tim was also one of the groomsmen for my wedding to Pam. He was the President of the Benziger family winery at the time—which sold in 2015—and still lives in beautiful Sonoma, California.

The year 1970 was a banner one for me in sports. In June of that year, I was awarded the General Excellence medal and the Scholar and Athlete Award from Iona Grammar School. I played on the varsity baseball and football teams. At the YMCA in Rye, where I swam in the winter, I was named co-captain of the team. I loved my coach, Jack Geagon, who had a great personal whistle that he used to help us with our stroke tempo. That year our team won the league, Westchester County, and NY State Championships. Also, on August 17, 1970, *The Daily Times* of Mamaroneck reported that I "put on one of the most impressive performances ever seen in the history of the Harbor Island Kiwanis Swim Meet yesterday with a first-place finish in the boys' freestyle, butterfly, backstroke, and breaststroke." It is still amazing to me because breaststroke was my worst event. I swam the Individual Medley throughout high school and college. The IM, as it's called, covers all four strokes in the following order: butterfly, backstroke, breaststroke, and freestyle. I would have to get as far ahead as possible during the first two legs of the swim just to finish strong.

I liked my time at Iona and I guess the Brothers did well on the preparatory part because they encouraged me to apply to a private boarding school for high school. I was accepted by and attended Phillips Andover Academy for my four years of high school. Andover was (and, I believe, still is) the best private boarding high school in the country. I give most of the credit to my Mother for my application to Andover. She was always very involved in my education, and always wanted the very best for me. She also made the best apple pie I have ever eaten. She was an incredible woman with many talents.

Andover was like a foreign country for me. My parents couldn't afford the full tuition, so I was on a combination scholarship and financial aid package. I'm not sure I was ever out of New York state prior to arriving in Andover, Massachusetts in September

1970 at the ripe old age of 13 (almost 14), except for the times we had been to Niagra Falls and Washington DC as a family. I was completely intimidated. The campus was vast and spectacular, the signature building, Samuel Phillips Hall, known as "SamPhill" looked like the beautiful and imposing buildings in Washington, DC. Still, I acclimated quickly to Andover and living away from home never bothered me.

Because of Andover's reputation and standards, everything about Andover was competitive and the students who matriculated there were the best of the best. Everyone seemed to have been number one in their academic class and captain of their sports teams. Even though several of my classmates were very wealthy, I never felt intimidated by them. I had always been at the top of my class academically and had always been a very good athlete and fit in well. I can honestly say that the rich kids never acted like rich kids and money was never an issue while I was at Andover. Andover was an all boys' school until 1973. Our graduating class of 1974 was the first co-educational class in the history of the school. The girls came from Abbot Academy, one of the finest private girls' schools in the country. Since the Abbott campus was just down the road from Andover, we often had classes in both places. During my junior and senior years, I always tried to have lunch on the Abbot campus... for the academic stimulation of course.

Two of the girls that I tried to have lunch with most often were Val Corning and Dana Delany. Val was model-beautiful and very smart and Dana, too, was incredibly beautiful and incredibly talented. Why they were hanging out with me, I didn't know; but I was smart enough not to fight it. Dana always wanted to be an actress and, during our senior year, played Nellie Forbus, the lead character in *South Pacific*, in our annual Spring performance. Dana went on to Hollywood fame in the role of Colleen McMurphy on the hit show *China Beach*, which ran for four seasons, and starred in great movies like *Tombstone* with Kurt Russell and Val Kilmer. Pretty heady company. I also spent time with another beautiful woman, Betsy Gootrad, who was more into art and music than I was. We had a host of other celebrated people in the class of 1974. They included: jazz composer Bill Cunliff, software genius Peter Currie, writer Nate Lee, and sculptor Gar Waterman. Gar was very funny and always a wild man.

I knew that I wanted to join the swimming team for the winter and the baseball team for spring. Andover had a trimester study curriculum and I was required to play a sport each season, so I decided to join the cross country team for the fall. Cross country basically tests how fast you can run a 5K (3.2 miles) over hill and dale and through the forest. I had never run more than 100 yard sprint so this was a challenge and a good test for me. I was a fast runner and made the team all four years. We had some really great runners, but I was usually in the first third of the pack. It was a great way to stay in good shape for swimming. One of the best cross country runners was Doug Greef, who became a pretty good friend. Doug was a very classy guy from New York City. I remember visiting him in his huge apartment near Park Avenue in the '70s. I really liked New York and secretly wished that I lived there, too.

Swimming is a winter sport at Andover and I would often have to get up in the bitter cold to go to practice. We had an excellent team and I'm sure that we beat Exeter, our biggest competitor, more often than they beat us. At Andover I swam the 100-yard Butterfly, the 100-yard Freestyle and the 400-yard Individual Medley, even though I still wasn't as good at breaststroke. The teammate I remember most from my swimming days at Andover was John Kingery. John had white-blond hair and was a year younger than me. He was the star of our team.

Spring was baseball time and I loved the sport. My Father was a big New York Yankees fan and on special occasions he would take me to a Yankees game. I loved going to Yankee Stadium with my Father. It was such a special place. The players were larger than life in their pinstripe uniforms and I loved spending time with my Father. I became a big Yankees fan too, and have always loved them; conversely, that meant that I had to hate The New York Mets. I remember often being in my bed at night with a small transistor radio listening to Phil Rizzuto calling the game. Mickey Mantle was a great home run hitter and my favorite player. I still remember the tall Mel Stottlemyre and the tough Jim Bouton pitching at the Stadium. To this day I am still a diehard Yankees fan.

My freshman year at Andover I was on the junior varsity baseball team. By my sophomore (lower) year I had made the varsity team. Even though I was still small, about 5'5", I was a pitcher and could throw hard. I also could throw a reasonably good curve ball. Andover's newspaper had a weekly Athlete of the Week section and I was Athlete of the Week twice in my junior (upper) year and once in my senior year. I remember two players in particular, Lennie Moher and Danny DiLorati, who were both very good players. Danny was a big hitter and all-around talented player. We had solid teams throughout my time at Andover and I'm sure we beat Exeter more than we lost to them.

I liked going to my classes during my years at Andover and had truly talented teachers. As you might expect, all the classes were challenging and making the grade was difficult. I remember having Ms. Bayard for French. Although I can still order dinner in a French restaurant, the only other thing I really can say in French is "La plume de ma tante" or "The pen of my aunt." My favorite classes were History and English. My favorite English teacher was Dr. Goodyear. I thought that Dr. Goodyear really cared about my education. He was an intellectual, and not at all athletic. We would occasionally go to his house for class, which was a fun way to change things up. Dr. Goodyear got me into F. Scott Fitzgerald, Ernest Hemmingway,

Gertrude Stein, and Ayn Rand—still my favorite novelists. In fact, I just gave my sons *The Fountainhead* and *Atlas Shrugged*, by Ayn Rand, as gifts for Christmas. He also introduced me to poetry and my favorite poet, T.S. Eliot. The end of my yearbook quote comes from *The Waste Land* by T.S. Eliot, one of the most influential poets of the 20TH century...

> Phillips Academy is an enormous, diverse family encompassing various facets of intellectuality and primitiveness, illusion and reality, regression and progress. Like any other family there are times to be happy and times to be sad, times to be together and times to be alone, never a time to feel pity for yourself and, most important, never a time not to smile. "Datta. Dayadhvam. Damyata. From What the Thunder Said: Give, Sympathize, Control."

I did well academically at Andover and got a good score on the SAT. I applied Early Decision to Williams College after visiting the picturesque campus and meeting with the exceptional swimming coach Carl Samualson. It was ranked as the No.1 Liberal Arts College in the nation. I was accepted. I was still swimming competitively during the summer between high school and college and was honored by the Larchmont Shore Club as the "outstanding competitor" that year. In June of that year I also won the 100 Butterfly event at the New York Athletic Club in NY in a record-setting time.

Being away for school at Williams was a lot easier for me after being at Andover for four years. Living away from home with a roommate became second nature. Williams is an idyllic place. Nestled in the far west corner of Northern Massachusetts the Williams campus is always touted as one of the most beautiful college campuses in the country. It is surrounded by the spectacular "Purple Mountains." So purple that our team color was purple and the Williams team mascot is the ferocious Purple Cow. It makes a great logo, even if it doesn't exactly strike fear into our opponents.

Pam and I still try to visit Williams at least once a year to play golf at the beautiful and challenging Taconic Golf Club, my favorite golf course in the world, which I was smart enough to join in 1987. We just love to walk around the campus and go to our favorite coffeehouse, Tunnel City, for cappuccinos and Americanos and have dinner at our favorite restaurant, Mezze. Ironically Pam went to Skidmore College, graduated in 1984, and loves going to Williamstown as much as I do. I say ironic because we would "road trip" from Williams to Skidmore in New York often to party with the women there. This had been a tradition for Williams men for decades. Skidmore is in Saratoga Springs and was much more of a party town than Williamstown, with great bars and restaurants on every corner.

Because of my injury, I unfortunately don't remember very much about my academic time at Williams. I was an English major and studied hard. My classmates were all brilliant and I *had* to study hard, just to keep up in that academically competitive environment. I must have enjoyed my classes and done relatively well. I was on the swimming team all four years. Our big competitor was Amherst, another great New England School and I think we beat them all four years that I was there. My coach was Carl Samualson, referred to simply as "Coach Sam" or the "Sammer." The Sammer was then and still is just amazing. I generally swam the 200-yard Butterfly and 200-yard Freestyle. During my college years I had my share of victories, but was not nearly the same swimming star as I had been when I was younger. Many of my teammates were just fantastic. My two favorite teammates were John Farmakis, a great overall swimmer from Connecticut, and RJ Connolly, a great freestyle sprinter from Buffalo, New York. We spent a lot of our free time at The Log, a school-run bar and the only bar within a few miles of the campus. The Log is at the end of Spring Street, the only main street in Williamstown. We spent many evenings there eating pretzels and drinking pitchers of beer. This was before eating pretzels and drinking a lot of beer was deemed harmful to our performance as swimmers.

In the winter of all four years, our entire varsity swimming team went to Ft. Lauderdale to practice at the Hall of Fame pool there. It was an awesome facility and we had a great time. It was a true Olympic-style facility, a bit different from our 6-lane, 25-yard pool (surrounded by dark walls) at Williams. Today, of course, Williams has an incredible swimming facility that would make UCLA jealous. It is named, appropriately, after The Sammer and Robert Muir, another legendary Williams swimming coach. Pam and I were able to go see The Sammer recently at the new pool facility along with John Farmakis, RJ Connelly and Paul Vom Eigen—another teammate of ours, a strong breaststroke specialist and great guy— at our 35TH class reunion. Of course, in Ft. Lauderdale, we had a curfew since we had to get up to swim at 8 a.m. every day. A curfew which, of course, we broke every night. We knew that we were not going to the Olympics, so we thought it was okay. This was a great perk that Williams provided.

CHAPTER 4

I also played water polo in the spring of all four of my years at Williams. A fantastic team sport and excellent exercise. It was fun to be able to play a truly "team" sport, after swimming all winter and I loved scoring goals. I still love watching water polo in the Summer Olympics.

My favorite non-academic activity at Williams was the annual Trivia Contest that occurred on the last night of both the winter and spring terms. Each dorm became its own team, and everyone would participate. The contest didn't start until 6:00 p.m. at night and would continue until 6:00 a.m. the next morning. Everyone in our dorm would gather in the common room where we had a bank of phones, pillows, boxes of pizza, at least two kegs of beer, and (of course) a good radio. The contest was hosted by the radio DJs of the previous year's winning team. This was well before the time of the internet and computers, so people would actually have to know the answers to the questions on their own. Basically, the contest sponsors would play a song and ask a trivia question. We would have to call in with the answers within three minutes. There also were one-hour and two-hour contests that didn't always involve trivia. My favorite challenge one year was to bring a Cub Scout in uniform to the hosting team's radio station. The faculty was aware of the contest and a favorite professor was not surprised when we showed up on his doorstep at 2:00 a.m. to seize his 10-year-old son to come with us. It was great fun and, like everything at Williams, very competitive. The winning dorm had the honor of hosting and defining the contest for the following year. My dorm never had that opportunity, but the competition sparked my love for trivia, which I still have today.

As I was getting ready to graduate during the spring of 1978, I couldn't decide what my next path would be.

While I had been a little arrogant (though a pretty nice guy) coming out of Iona, all my classmates at Andover and Williams were also the smartest student and the best athlete in their classes and I had to realize that I was no longer the best or brightest at everything. It was humbling, but also a great experience for me. In retrospect, it made me a stronger person with higher standards for myself. It made me work harder to succeed.

I knew I wanted to continue to Graduate School, but I was not sure whether the path should be Business School or Law School. My grades were reasonably good at Williams and I graduated with a degree in English. I decided that Law School was the better path for me. I always loved watching *Perry Mason* on TV when I was younger and loved logical reasoning. I also thought that Law School would be a better place to continue being challenged at writing and other cognitive skills. And I loved, and still love, to argue my positions—it's the Irish way. I wanted to be in New York for law school. I loved my time both at Andover and Williams and really think that both places had very positive influences on my life. Living away from home for eight years had also helped me mature and become a more independent person.

Since my Father was not in the best of health, I thought it would be good for all of us if I was closer to home. The two best Law Schools in New York were NYU Law and Fordham Law. I think I applied and was accepted at both schools, but decided on Fordham. It had a solid reputation for helping students get jobs in good law firms and was located right in the center of the City at Lincoln Center. Once I made that choice, I also knew that I wanted to live in New York City. I had made some money over the years coaching swimming and was going to return to Larchmont Yacht Club for my fourth season as head coach that summer. I had two good friends from Williams who also wanted to live in NYC. One was Frank Carr, who was going to work for a major bank, and John Farmakis, my swimming teammate, who went to work for a major advertising firm.

Since I was a student and supposedly had more free time, I was enlisted to find an apartment for the three of us. For almost two weeks I scoured *The New York Times* and walked the streets of the West Side (which I knew would be more affordable than the East Side) until I found something that sounded (and was) perfect. It was a fantastic three-bedroom, three-bathroom apartment in a full-service, doorman-operated building at 12 West 72ND Street just steps from Central Park West and Central Park and right across the street from the famous Dakota. The building was called the Oliver Cromwell and the asking rent was only $1,200 per month. (I think the apartment would rent for at least $7,000 per month today.) This was well before the era of cell phones, but I reached both John and Frank at their offices and told them that we had to meet that night to look at the apartment right away. We met at the iconic Paddy McGlade's bar on 67TH and Columbus, which became a regular haunt for us through Law School. Unfortunately, McGlades, after more than 100 years in business, did not survive the gentrification of the Upper West Side and my good friends from Law School, Bill Macdonald, Cort Delany and Scott Garley made it to McGlade's bar for cheeseburgers and a few pints of Guinness just before it closed in 2012.

After dinner we went to see the apartment. I was very glad that we didn't let any more time pass. We were immediately impressed that the building had two doormen and went to the 12TH floor. The apartment was spectacular. It had a huge living room, a dining room and a full kitchen and three spacious bedrooms, each with its own bathroom. The boys and I could barely believe our luck and signed the lease that night. We had the nicest apartment of all our friends and always had people coming by (and staying over). We threw great parties in that apartment. It still may be one of the best personal real estate deals that I've done in my career, and my career has been doing real estate deals. The Oliver Cromwell became a cooperative apartment building during my time there. Just for fun, I wanted to see if any apartments were now available. I found a two-bedroom for an asking price of $1.6 million. I would imagine that our apartment today would be worth at least $2 million. To put it in perspective, my last apartment in Manhattan, in 2011 and 2012, was a very large one-bedroom rental on the Upper East side. It was great—but not nearly as great as "12/12," as we had called it. How the mighty have fallen. I gave up the Oliver Cromwell apartment when I got married on August 22, 1981 to my beautiful girlfriend Peggy Daniel. It was a good trade.

Except for that great apartment, my roommates, and a few good friends I remember very little about my time at Fordham Law. I do know that Fordham Law is at Lincoln Center and was within easy walking distance from my apartment. We spent a lot of time at McGlade's and, according to my good friends, I never went to class. These friends were Bill Macdonald, Scott Garley, Cort Delany, and John Ciraldo. John passed away a few years ago, way too young. Scott and Cort all are managing partners in prestigious law firms; Scott in NYC and Cort in Connecticut. Bill is a successful movie producer in Hollywood, California best known for his work on the movie *Sliver* (with Sharon Stone and Michael Douglas) and the successful television series *Rome*. He is now working on a new series about New Orleans in the Roaring Twenties. Bill is both the writer and the producer of the show. I still see Cort and Scott whenever we visit New York and Bill whenever we visit LA and we always have a great time together.

On the evening of December 8, 1980, the West Side of New York and the entire world was rocked by the murder of John Lennon, the leader and founder of The Beatles. He was shot in the vestibule of the Dakota apartment building where he lived with his wife, Yoko Ono. I was in my apartment that night with my roommates and Peggy having a pasta dinner. To this day, Peggy is convinced that she heard the shots that night. Between the police response and the number of Lennon and Beatles fans who came in the thousands, our neighborhood was bedlam for months. During that time, I needed to show an ID just to get into my apartment.

CHAPTER 5

My Mother died on March 15, 1981 during my final year at Fordham. I was devastated. It was the worst day of my life. My Mother was my rock. She was the smartest woman I have ever known; she taught me how to think, to dress, to dance, to laugh, and how to be a good person. I gave her eulogy about the Ides of March at Most Holy Trinity Church. It was the first time I had ever spoken to an audience without notes. I've spoken in public many times since that day and always think of my Mom when I do. I have never been nervous speaking with her by my side.

I had to finish my last year at Fordham for her. I really wish I'd had more time with her. I know that she would have liked to have seen me graduate. I also know it would have made me a better person. She was an incredible person and role model.

After a few weeks of all-nighters to get all my papers and other work done, I managed to graduate in the top 20% of my class at Fordham. This was anathema to my close friends who are still quite sure that I never went to class. After graduating in May 1981, the real work started: studying for the Bar Exam.

The five of us knew one thing for certain: we wanted to take the Bar Exam only once. We decided to work together to make that happen. One of the smartest things I did in Law School was to join The New York Athletic Club on 60TH and Central Park West, not far from my apartment and also very close to Fordham. Every morning starting in July 1981 the five of us would meet at the Fordham library with coffee and bagels at around 9:00 a.m. and start reading documents required for the test. At around 1:00 p.m.

Billy and I would go to the NYAC and play pick-up basketball with other former college athletes trying to stay in shape. Many of these guys had played basketball in college which (together with my towering height) put me at a bit of a disadvantage. I'm all of 5'7" and was never tall enough to think seriously about playing the game very well. I was fast, however, and had decent defensive skills as well as an okay set shot. I learned a lot about the game from the good players and it was a great way to stay focused between study sessions. Exercise always is good for a little additional brain power.

In my last year of law school I also got hooked on playing squash at the NYAC. Squash had all the things that I loved in a sport. It's a very fast-paced racquet sport that requires speed, good eye-hand coordination, and involves single competition. I played as often as I could. I got reasonably good and played in as many tournaments as I could. I'm pretty sure that I won more than I lost.

We would spend almost every night, after studying, at McGlade's trying to kill as many brain cells as possible by drinking beer all night to make studying the next morning as difficult as possible.

The days before the Bar Exam were pretty intense—so much so that the five of us stopped drinking for the entire week before we took the exam in September of 1981. It was a two-day test and after the first day we all thought that we might as well have been drinking for the week. It was, by far, the most difficult day in my educational career and the most difficult test I had ever taken. We all spent the evening studying more. After we completed the exam the next day, we made up for our week of not drinking. We spent the night at McGlade's drowning our sorrows in Guinness and Amstel Light. As it turns out, we all (amazingly) passed the exam the first time and received our Juris Doctorate degrees in late 1981. All five of us were admitted to the Bar of The State of New York on June 21, 1982, by the Appellate Division, First Judicial Department.

Why we selected a bareboat sailing trip to celebrate our new careers, I still don't know. But we did. We decided to go to Bimini, a small island in the Caribbean. I also invited my younger brother, Tim to join us. So, in early September 1981, six of us (with John Ciraldo also joining the party) set sail from Miami to Bimini, about 50 nautical miles away. None of us had ever been to the Caribbean before, but we wanted to do something that was a bit exotic and out of our comfort zone. Cort, Bill, and John had been sailing before and also had some experience in navigation. Scott, Tim, and I were complete novices to the sport, but we were good at drinking beer. To save money, since we had been law students for the past three years, we decided to drive to Miami where we had made arrangements to rent the boat. We took turns driving, sleeping, and eating and made it to Florida in about a day.

When we arrived at the marina, Cort, Bill, and John were given the task of securing our vessel while Scott, Tim, and I were put on provisioning detail. Of course, we loaded up on beer and snack food. I'm not sure what Cort and Bill said to the owner of the boat to allow us to take it out, but it must have been convincing. We got a beautiful 32-foot sloop called *The Katherine* and off we went. About 24 hours, 50 nautical miles, and several beers later we were at the dock in Bimini at the Bimini Bay Club near Alice Town, Bahamas.

Today the Bimini Bay Resort and Marina is a 3-Star Resort. That was not the case in 1981. The hotel was clean and right on the Caribbean Sea and had a great bar near the beach with music at night. To celebrate the fact that we had made it to Bimini without incident, we drank a few beers, and danced with the guests every night. The only story that I really remember from Bimini is the "Crazy Bimini Lady" escapade. Although Cort appeared to be the most harmless of our group, he is in fact completely devious in a hilarious way. We may never know exactly what went on at the hotel bar that night with the Crazy Bimini Lady—who, of course, had a very Bahamian accent and chanted and danced in front of us and said that we all would be forever cursed. So, we all have that going for us; which is nice.

We had four great days of sun, sand, and the Caribbean Sea… and then it was time to head home. We figured that if we could find Bimini in the middle of the Atlantic Ocean and the Caribbean we could find the dock in Fort Lauderdale on the return trip. And we did. As we had on the entire way to Bimini, we listened to reggae music by Bob Marley, Jimmy Cliff (better known as Jimmy Spliff) and Toots and the Maytals leading the way for us. And, of course, we drank as much beer as we could. We arrived back in Miami on a beautiful sunny day and headed for the dock and boat rental area we had left from. Once again, I was amazed and impressed that we had hit the mark and give great credit to Bill, John, and Cort. Of course, the owner of *The Katherine* was on the dock to greet us as we drove the boat aground, not once, but twice just before reaching the dock. There was no damage to the boat, so we got our full security deposit back. The owner just laughed at us and bought us a beer after we disembarked. We had an unbelievable trip and it was great to be able to spend some time with Tim.

During my days at Andover, Williams, and Fordham, in addition to studying all the time (yeah right) I really got interested in three things—Rock and Roll music from the '60s and '70s which I always listened to while studying, classic movies, and trivia-logic puzzles. I still love all three today and still try to keep my brain stimulated by reading logic books and doing logic puzzles every day. It drives Pam crazy that I can still name almost every song and artist on the radio as we listen to Classic Rock in the car, but I can't remember the details of our wedding.

After graduating from Fordham and being admitted to the New York Bar, I joined the prestigious firm of Sage, Gray, Todd & Simms in late 1981. Sage Gray introduced me to the area of real estate law, which became my specialty. They also taught me how to work in an office environment. I was so excited about passing the bar that I asked my gorgeous girlfriend, Peggy, to marry me, and she made the mistake of saying Yes. Peggy was working at Bank of America at the time and on her way to a very successful career. Peggy is from a prominent suburb of St. Louis. Her father, Peyton, was a very successful insurance executive with a great personality and his wife, Jane, was very active in charitable work in St. Louis. We were married in St. Louis on August 22, 1981 with my brother Tim as best man, Peggy's sister Christin as her maid of honor, and Peggy's brother Peyton as one of my ushers. Even though I am Irish Catholic we were married in an Episcopalian Church (Peggy is Episcopalian—and her Dad was paying for the wedding). The Daniels were kind enough to allow me to also have a Catholic Priest be part of the service. I understand that it was a wonderful and very fun event, but I really don't remember. In addition to Tim as my best man, Cort, Scott, and Bill were my ushers. Of course, we had to light up St. Louis for a few days, but no one got arrested and the wedding came off well. We got the nickname "the wrecking crew" from the local crowd. Peggy and I went to Bermuda for our honeymoon. I'm sure that we had an awesome time. It was my second trip to the Caribbean in just a few months and I loved it. Little did I know then that I was destined to do a lot of work in the Caribbean.

We lived in New York City for several years, but we wanted to start a family. We started to look for homes in Westchester County where I was born and where I was very familiar with the area. The home prices were ridiculously high, and we looked for alternatives. One of Peggy's friends was living in a suburb called Upper Montclair, New Jersey so we looked for homes there. We found a great four-bedroom house, with a pool (which I particularly liked) for much less than the home prices in Larchmont or Rye or anywhere in Westchester County we had looked. The house was situated up on a hill and in the winter we could see NYC through the bare trees. We moved to that house in Upper Montclair in 1986; the house that Peggy still lives in with her husband Gregg. I joined the Montclair Golf Club in late 1988. It's a very nice club with three 9-hole courses and punishing greens. I played there often and got to be a single-digit handicap golfer by 1995.

My brother Tim must have seen how well my marriage was going, so he decided to get married too. He married the lovely and talented Siobhan Regan, his longtime girlfriend on June 18, 1988 at the Larchmont Yacht Club. I was his best man and I am told that it was an awesome wedding. Tim and Siobhan will be celebrating their 30TH wedding anniversary next year. It's amazing what love can do. I'm sure that my being Tim's best man brought them good luck.

CHAPTER 6

From the beginning at Sage Gray I was assigned a secretary who took dictation. It was a great learning experience for me. I had never learned to type very well but got very good at dictating correspondence. Since I had secretaries all throughout my legal career, by the time I left my last firm I could even dictate short documents like notes and short contracts from memory. Dictation was a great way to learn how to organize thoughts quickly and concisely and gave me confidence in public speaking.

Since we worked very hard, I took an opportunity for a little levity on October 29, 1982 to circulate a memo to all the lawyers entitled "Halloween Costumes We'd Like to See." Looking back, it was a pretty ballsy move, since I had only been at the firm about a year. I gave each lawyer in the firm a costume and the memo was well received. My costume was "Popeye." And I'm not stupid, I made the Senior Partner of the firm who I really liked, "God."

I left Sage Gray in early 1983 and went to Schulte, Roth & Zabel, a smaller, boutique firm. At SRZ I again routinely worked 14 hours a day, as I did throughout my whole legal career. SRZ was started in 1969 by three young, aggressive lawyers, Steve Schulte, Paul Roth and Bill Zabel. My time at SRZ was great. When I started there I initially spent a lot of time with Paul Roth, who was a brilliant lawyer and leader and really taught me how to be a good lawyer. I started to focus on a real estate transactional practice and worked closely with Paul Nussbaum who, at a very young age, was already a partner and head of the real estate practice for the firm. He was great to work with and taught me all about being a good real estate lawyer. Paul taught me how to close deals and I quickly began to handle significant and complex corporate real estate deals as well as residential deals. My practice involved mostly sophisticated corporate sale and purchase transactions which allowed me to learn about tough negotiation tactics as well as high-level financing. We did deals involving large commercial companies and hotels. This practice taught me how to read and understand complex contracts and financing documents and how to negotiate both pricing and financing transactions. My first closing was a $20 million office building in New York that also involved a $16 million loan. I was involved in almost every aspect of the deal and it was very exciting for me to be part of the team. I really liked closing real estate deals because (unlike litigation) both parties are generally trying to seek the same result. I loved negotiating and closing deals where, most often, both parties walked away from the table feeling good. And I also really liked that a closing generally was followed by a champagne celebration.

At SRZ I also met John Fallon, an intelligent, tough and, (like me) ambitious young Irishman. John became a very close friend and was one of my ushers at my wedding to Pam in Phoenix in 1999. John specialized in corporate, takeover, and tax transactions. Sadly, over the last few years, I have lost touch with John, but I always will be most grateful to him for teaching me how to play golf. John lived in Long Island and was a member of a very nice golf club in Garden City. Like me, John had been an accomplished athlete through high school and college and he had started playing golf at a young age. I was pathetic the first few times we played, using my baseball swing and seeing poor results. But (as you may have gathered already) I am very competitive, particularly concerning sports, and I continued to improve as I played more. John was a great teacher, and a very good golfer, and my years of playing baseball and swimming had given me good balance and good eye-hand coordination. And did I mention that I was very competitive?

Within the first year of playing I broke 100 and by my third year I was shooting in the high 80s on a regular basis. I really appreciated, and still appreciate, that John worked with me so much and took me to play twice a month during the summers that we worked together. John and I worked on a few deals together and would often find ourselves in Paul Roth's office at the same time. Paul was intense and taught us a lot, and was very nice to us. He would ask very salient questions about our work—questions that we often couldn't answer very well, but knew his intention was to make us better lawyers.

I really liked working at SRZ and put in long hours. Work at law firms generally starts about 10:00 a.m., so generally I didn't have to get up at the crack of dawn. However, I rarely left the office before midnight. But long hours aside, I loved my work. Because I was so hard-working I was given a lot of responsibility and got the opportunity to work on several high-profile deals. My Mother had a big influence on my success. Being the seamstress for many wealthy businessmen, she knew how important "dressing for success" really is. So, with my limited savings, I bought two Zegna suits and five Hermès ties and always wore cuff links to work. I don't think it was lost on some of the partners at SRZ and my other firms that I was dressing better than they were. John loved to call my suits my "Ziggy Diggy" suits to the partners. From then on and to this day I have only bought Zegna, Armani and Canali suits and jackets, Hermès ties and still love to wear cuff links when we go out to special events.

I always felt, and still feel, that wearing great clothes helped me a lot with my confidence in negotiations and, generally, in life. I've also always felt that my clients were more comfortable with a lawyer who always dressed well because I think that it gave them a sense of confidence, too. In addition to quality suits and ties, my Mother also told me to look at a man's shoes to get a sense of the type of person he is. It seems superficial, but I've found that men who wear great shoes are more successful. To this day I always wear only business shoes made in England or Italy.

I am still not sure why I left SRZ in late 1986. I consider it one of the biggest mistakes that I've made in my career. It must have been related to money. In 1986 SRZ was still a relatively small boutique firm that paid slightly less than most of the bigger firms. I went to Winthrop, Simpson, one of those big name, "white-shoe" firms in New York. I really liked the people at Winthrop, Simpson, but never felt 100 percent comfortable there. For some reason I felt that it would take me longer than I wanted to make partner. I left Winthrop, Simpson in early 1988 after a little more than a year and joined the firm of Townley & Updike, where they said I could head their real estate practice even as a senior associate and promised a quick path to partnership if I performed well.

I worked most closely with a partner named Mark Geraghty, who also become a fast friend. It was at Townley that I closed the most exciting residential deal of my career. It was a NY condominium deal and my client was Isabella Rossellini, daughter of the famous actress Ingrid Bergman. Isabella and her husband Jon Weidemann were referred to me by my brother-in-law, Peyton. The deal, thankfully, was closed without incident and Isabella and Jon were very happy. *Casablanca* is, in my opinion, the best movie of all time. It was an incredible honor for me to talk to Isabella about Humphrey Bogart, her Mother and *Casablanca* and to handle her real estate deal personally. It also probably wasn't lost on the partners that I had done a successful deal with a famous client.

CHAPTER 7

During this time came the happiest day of my life: the birth of my son Ian on September 26, 1988. It was magical for me. And I decided it was time to change my career.

I really liked being a lawyer, but I decided that I would rather be a client than a lawyer. I had learned that being on the other side of a deal was potentially a lot more lucrative and better for my family as a lifestyle choice. I wanted to find a position where I could be a principal and still use my legal expertise in a corporate career where I could negotiate deals for myself.

The next happiest day of my life came on March 10, 1992 with the birth of my son Riley. The feeling of having a second son was amazing. But now, I really needed to get to work. And I got lucky once again. I was playing golf every weekend at Montclair Golf Club with two people who had become very good friends: David DiBrigida and Tom Higgins. David was a few years younger than me, a Lehigh graduate, a varsity college hockey player, a lawyer, and a single digit handicap golfer. He had already helped my game a lot. Tom was a few years older than me and was already a partner in a prestigious New York law firm. He was about a 15-handicap golfer and one of the funniest people I have ever met. We would have a great time drinking beers and eating pretzels after a round. I told both David and Tom that I was looking for a job that could combine my legal skills with a corporate career and Tom said he thought he had something that might be perfect for me. He was friends with a fellow named Andy Jubelt who was the president of a boutique real estate firm in New York called Affirmative Equities and was looking for someone who could provide both legal and real estate experience to his firm.

I liked Andy right away and we got along very well. He had an office on Wooster Street in Soho and we agreed on a deal almost immediately. Affirmative was managing several multi-family housing projects in Northern New Jersey at the time and owned a boutique hotel in Roanoke, Virginia named "The Patrick Henry." The office was divided into two sections. One had a few accountants working on property management and the other was for real estate deals. Affirmative had three other employees at the time: Marty Beard, the "numbers guy," Ariadne Bender, a very talented young lawyer, and Bill McLaughry, a smart businessman. Andy was a great squash player which added to the fun. I would drive in from New Jersey every morning, we would play squash at the local gym and then get to work. Andy was also like me, very competitive, and playing with him made me a better player, for which I am forever grateful.

Andy also had an apartment in Soho and two beautiful black Bouvier des Flanders dogs. A Bouvier is almost as large as Mastiff but as gentle as a Golden Retriever. Andy also had a lake house in New Jersey, so the dogs could run on weekends. Andy had several beautiful Persian rugs in his apartment and the office. He introduced me to a store in Pennsylvania that sold authentic Persian rugs at much reduced prices to New York. I went there with him several times and bought several great Persian rugs.

At Affirmative we all liked to drink a little and were a very collegial group, so we often went out together after work. Soho is a great place to work and play. Our two favorite haunts were Barolo, a fabulous Italian restaurant, and I Tre Merli, a great casual bar that Marty and I often went to together. We also traveled to play golf. I had planned a golf trip to Las Vegas with my brother, John Fallon, and Marty. We stayed at the Desert Inn. It was great to spend a little time with my brother. We played golf and gambled for two days and had a fabulous time.

At the office, Andy and I needed to hire a new assistant and I was tasked with the job of finding one. I went to our headhunting agency for applicants. The most impressive resume I received came from Pamela Pillone. She had graduated from Skidmore College and had recently graduated from Fordham Business School (both serendipitously) which she had attended at night while working as a buyer at Tiffany & Co. She passed my typing test with ease and most impressive was that she knew how to run analytics on the Bloomberg Terminal that we had in our office. The Bloomberg Terminal was, at the time, perhaps the most revered and iconic tool of financial markets, connecting market participants with industry data and analytics long before the era of the Internet. Little did I know when I interviewed Pam that she would become my wife and the love of my life. I just knew that she was beautiful, very overqualified and perfect for the job. Pam recalls that I was wearing a full three-piece Italian suit with an Hermès tie and she commented on how nice I looked and what a contrast it was to our 'artsy' Soho loft office. I told her that I got dressed up just for her. We still joke about the fact that she believed me. Pam became a senior analyst for us shortly after she joined the firm.

Not long after Pam joined the firm, Andy wanted to start a REIT—a Real Estate Investment Trust. I had some experience with REITs from my days as a lawyer and knew that we needed a much larger property portfolio than The Patrick Henry and a very large financial investor to be successful. I thought that success would be a long shot.

Andy and I parted amicably, and I started Stonebridge Group and took great office space overlooking the ice skating rink at Rockefeller Center. Marty, Bill McLaughry, and Pam joined Stonebridge with me. We had three deals in the works at

Stonebridge, and the first was a deal brought by Bill. Bill's wife was a doctor at NYU and there were four in-vitro doctors who were unhappy with their current situation. I was able to negotiate a much better financial deal for them to move their practice to St. Barnabas Hospital. The second deal involved Joyce Geiger. I had met Joyce when we were both speaking at a Real Estate conference and was very impressed with her. She is one of the most brilliant real estate professionals I have ever met, and I have met a lot of very smart people in the industry. She had started a company named Reitrac, which became the industry standard in analyzing REITs, and she engaged me to successfully negotiate and close the sale of her company to Teleres. Joyce is still a great friend of mine and Pam's today and someone we love to spend time with when we are in New York. The other significant deal involved Paine Webber, which, I believe, also came to us from a speaking engagement. Paine Webber hired me and Stonebridge to do due diligence on a portfolio of multi-family properties across the country. Paine Webber even gave us office space in their Wall Street offices to do the work. We would often go to the famous Fraunces Tavern after work for a bite and a cocktail. Located on the corner of Pearl Street and Broad Street, Fraunces Tavern is one of the oldest restaurants in NYC. It was built in 1719, and it was magnificent. It was there that George Washington said farewell to his troops after the Revolutionary War. Paine Webber was interested in buying and eventually selling the "B" piece of a larger Commercial Mortgage Backed Security (CMBS) bond portfolio. (See the movie *The Big Short* to get a better idea about CMBS portfolios and why due diligence is so important for an investor.) The properties we were tasked with reviewing were mostly in the Western part of the country. We split up into two teams and with Pam on my team, we took the Southwest. After completing our due diligence tour of such exciting places as El Paso and Tucson over the course of about 10 days, I wanted to celebrate a little, so

I booked rooms at the 5-Star Arizona Biltmore Hotel, which was designed by my favorite architect, Frank Lloyd Wright.

While I was at the Biltmore, the hotel was advertising the construction and sale of new condominium Villas. Always curious about real estate opportunities, I took a tour of the Villa model. It was spectacular. To make it even more compelling, I knew the broker who was running the sales and marketing for the Villas. She told me that this was an incredible opportunity, and she was right. The Villa was a beautiful, fully furnished with furniture designed by Frank Lloyd Wright two-bedroom, 1,600-square foot condominium with a huge living area, vaulted ceilings, a fireplace, and an outdoor terrace spanning the entire Villa and overlooking the Paradise pool. What made it doubly appealing for me was that I could use the Villa for 60 days each year and the hotel would rent it out whenever possible, pool the proceeds from all other Villa rentals and pay me a percentage of the net profit from those proceeds every quarter. It also had a very large "owners closet" where we could secure clothes and other personal things like golf clubs under lock and key. I bought the Villa shortly thereafter.

I think that I have always been a generous person and often tried to match generosity with fun. In my two years at Stonebridge I continued a Christmas tradition that I had started at Affirmative. I rented a limousine for a day of window shopping at the best retail stores on Madison and Fifth Avenue and cocktails at great bars. Marty and I would start around lunchtime with several bottles of Veuve Cliquot and pick up and drop off friends and clients throughout the day. We would go to all the best retail stores like Armani, Fendi, Tiffany, and FAO Schwarz to look around and pretend we were big spenders and stop for cocktails at famed bars like the 21 Club, the Monkey Bar, and the Oak Room. We would end the day at the bar at The Penninsula with our favorite bartenders Sal and Al for one more glass of Veuve Cliquot.

CHAPTER 8

In 1993, Peggy and I agreed to divorce. It was emotionally devastating, but fairly amicable and I agreed to most of Peggy's requests. Peggy kept the house in Upper Montclair and I kept my Biltmore Villa. The boys would continue to live with Peggy. The thing I cared most about was keeping joint custody of the boys. She knew that I was a good father and we came to a reasonable compromise.

The Paine Webber deal was coming to an end and I needed a new job. I'm not sure how I reconnected with my former mentor from SRZ, Paul Nussbaum, but it was great that I did. Paul had become the CEO of Patriot American Hospitality, a public hospitality REIT in Dallas, Texas and he hired me as a Senior Vice President and Head of Acquisitions. By this time Pam and I were a couple and very much in love. Thankfully, Pam agreed to come with me and we moved to Dallas. We rented a great two-bedroom condominium in Los Colinas right next to the Four Seasons Hotel. The Four Seasons became our 'kitchen,' although we also liked to go to Star Canyon for a special dinner twice a month. Star Canyon was a fabulous restaurant with renowned Stephen Pyle as the chef-owner. The Four Seasons also had a great health club and squash courts, so I would play almost every day and played in several competitions. I loved it. The Four Seasons also had a tremendous championship golf course designed by the legendary Byron Nelson that held his namesake professional tournament for 15 years, including the years that we lived in Dallas. So, it was always great fun to go to the tournament and The Four Seasons always had special parties during the event. The course was public, so I could play every weekend.

Pam was able to join the Dallas Polo Club to continue her passion for riding which was awesome for both of us. She also did some work for Patriot, digitizing hard copies of due diligence files and converting entire file rooms to CD.

In 1996 Patriot was a sponsor of the Summer Olympics in Atlanta. Pam and I and Ian and Riley were able to go the games for four days and had a great time despite the pipe bombing on July 27TH that happened while we were there. We were staying in a suite in a hotel that Patriot owned at the time. Patriot had arranged for a very large suite with food and drinks for clients and had an array of tickets to various events. I loved the swimming events, Pam loved the equestrian events, and the boys just loved being there. They also loved having access to a limousine (with a television and loads of snacks) that took us to and from the hotel every day so we never missed anything. Our other favorite events were track and field where we got to see Michael Johnson (wearing his famed gold running shoes) compete and break the word record in the 200-meter dash and basketball where Dream Team Two won gold in the second Olympics that allowed professional players to compete. That year the team included Charles Barkley and Karl Malone. It was funny to see the U.S. team with its full cadre of trainers and strength coaches competing with what looked like college teams.

I soon met Bill Hooten a seasoned hotel broker, a good friend of Paul's, and a great golfer. We became fast friends. Bill was a member of the exclusive Preston Trail Golf Club, an all-male club. I got to play often with Bill at Preston Trail and loved it because the competition was always keen, and, unlike most other golf clubs, there were very few rules. He introduced me to a deal being brokered by a good friend of his in Phoenix named Bill Graham.

Bill Graham was best friends with Rusty Lyon, a very successful real estate entrepreneur who, among other things, owned a portfolio of fabulous luxury resorts in the West including The Boulders in Carefree, Arizona, The Peaks at Telluride in Telluride, Colorado, Ventana Canyon in Tucson, Arizona, and Carmel Valley Ranch in Carmel, California that he wanted to sell. It sounded like a great deal to me, so Bill Hooten and I flew to Phoenix to meet with Rusty and Bill Graham. Both were great guys and we all bonded quickly. I thought it would be great to add four 4-Star hotels to the Patriot portfolio of mostly 3-Star properties. The previous deal I had closed for Patriot was a portfolio of Doubletree Hotels.

I took the Carefree Portfolio deal to Paul and he also liked it right away. To his credit, he just told me to get it done. The due diligence was painful at times, having to spend time in Carefree, Telluride, and Carmel but I somehow managed. I spent a lot of time with the two Bills and Rusty in Phoenix which I loved, and Pam and I really became special friends with Bill Graham, who I can only describe as a truly incredible man. Through Bill Graham, Pam and I got to meet his wife Kerry, who is also a truly special person. Kerry is a professional golf instructor and had been the President of the LPGA (Ladies Professional Golf Association) Teaching and Club Professional Division from 1987 through 1993. Today she is one of our best friends.

We had significant competition for the Carefree deal, and our main competitor was confident that they would win. So confident that the senior acquisition team showed up at Rusty's office for a meeting in blue jeans and tee shirts, a bit too cool for school. Rusty was an awesome person, and not that type of guy. The Carefree deal went to me and Patriot.

The Closing Dinner for the Carefree Resorts acquisition was held at The Boulders on May 1, 1997. It was incredible. At the dinner, in his toast, Rusty thanked me personally for my work in closing the deal. It was not the most lucrative deal I have ever done personally but it still is the most special. The Murphys and the Grahams became such good friends that after the deal we spent every New Year's Eve together at the Biltmore Villa with Ian and Riley. Bill passed away on November 16, 2007, way too young, and Kerry remains one of our very best friends.

About the time that I closed the Carefree deal I was also involved in the purchase by Patriot of Wyndham Hotels. I didn't love the deal and told Paul that I would look for another job. I will always be grateful to Paul for giving me the job at Patriot and believing in me.

Pam and I stayed in Dallas for the next year and I took a position as Senior Vice President of Fidelity National Title Insurance Company working for Bob Calamari. I met Bob while working at Patriot. Every commercial real estate deal involves title insurance. Especially in sophisticated hotel deals, providing clear title is paramount to closing and often takes a sophisticated title agent. Bob is the best. We became close friends and I tried to use Bob in my real estate closings whenever possible.

Bob, like me, was an avid golfer and in the summer of 1988 he arranged the best boys' golf trip I have ever been a part of. It was called the Turnberry Cup because Bob and Fidelity arranged for me and 14 clients to travel to Scotland with Bob for four days to play the legendary Turnberry golf course. We played golf, gambled, drank a little scotch, and ate our share of haggis. On our last night we all wore kilts to the closing dinner and Bob arranged to have a bagpiper serenade us next to the 18TH green as we all drank our last glasses of scotch—neat, of course. It was truly fantastic, and Bob did a terrific job with the whole experience. I really wish I had a better memory of the event. On the final night, Bob gave us all a framed picture of the 16 of us in our kilts as a momento of the trip. I have that picture hanging in a special place in my house so I can look at it every day and smile.

In addition to golf trips, I loved playing in Member-Guest Tournaments. My two favorites were at Montclair Golf Club and Ardsley Country Club in Westchester. My brother Tim was always my partner at Montclair. I don't think we ever won at golf, but we always won at the poker table. Ardsley was a more competitive affair and my host and partner was Tony Altamura. Tony is a truly great guy and is also a very good golfer. He was my attorney for many years, until my injury. In the Ardsley tournament, like most Member-Guest tournaments, golfers compete in "flights" (usually four) based on a team's total handicap and the winners of each of the respective flights compete at the end of the tournament for the overall championship. Tony and I were always in the championship flight because we both had low handicaps. We won the overall trophy in 2006 in a playoff when I holed a sand wedge on the last hole. Since the green was elevated and I could not see the flag, I knew it was in when the crowd gave a roar as the ball went in. I think Tony and I got second place for each of the next four years. Ardsley always gave trophies that I still cherish.

When Pam hosted an event at Larchmont Yacht Club to commemorate the first anniversary of my injury, Tony and his wife Terri were there. Tony and Terri gave me a great leather wallet that I still use today to remember the day.

During my golfing career, I also played in my share of charity events. My favorite outing was in the summer of 2010 when I played with my friends from Montclair Golf Club and Saucon Valley, Dave DiBrigida and Mark McGowen. Dave and I were both good golfers; Mark was an exceptional golfer. Dave, Mark, and I were paired with the LPGA pro, Morgan Pressel. Morgan turned pro at age 17 and is the second youngest winner of a Major LPGA golf tournament. According to Dave, we had a great time, played reasonably well despite being totally intimidated by Morgan's impressive talent, and even got her to drink a shot of tequila with us at the 19TH hole. The fun of playing with great people is one of the main reasons I love golf. After my injury I promised Pam that my shot-drinking days were over.

In the winter after the Turnberry Cup I got a job as a Senior Vice President at Boykin Lodging Company in Cleveland, Ohio to help advance their acquisition practice. The CEO of BLC was Bob Boykin. I told Pam that night, "Honey, I have great news— we're moving to Cleveland." She said "Really? This should be interesting." And it was. I was hired as a Senior Vice President at BLC to augment their acquisition group. Like Patriot, BLC was a public hospitality REIT. Bob was gracious enough to put Pam and me into a hotel in town owned by BLC while we looked for a more permanent place to live. While living in the hotel we put all our furniture and most of our belongings into storage. In December of 1998 the storage facility burned to the ground. In addition to our furniture and a lot of expensive clothes, I had six Persian rugs that burned in the fire. The only silver lining was that Bob also had a lot of things in the same storage facility at the time of the fire, which made the resolution of our insurance claim a lot easier and a lot more expeditious.

Michael, Ian and Riley at Bill Macdonald's wedding • Italy 2004

Michael and Pam at the Bedford Post • New York 2010

Michael and Pam in South Hampton • New York 2010

*Michael standing and 20 pounds
lighter in Larchmont
• New York 2012 •*

*Michael, Ian, and Riley celebrating
Michael's birthday in Larchmont
• New York 2013 •*

CHAPTER 9

Pam and I always went back to New York for the Christmas holiday and I proposed marriage to her on Christmas Eve in 1988 in a suite at The Four Seasons. I got down on one knee and my ring was the top of a Veuve Clicquot champagne bottle. Since Pam had been a buyer at Tiffany for many years and is GIA certified in diamond grading, I knew better than to try to pick out a ring by myself. Thankfully she said Yes, and the happiest part of my life began.

We soon picked a ring and were married on March 13, 1999 at the Biltmore Hotel in Arizona. We had the rehearsal dinner at El Chorro the night before and the wedding on the main lawn of the Biltmore next to our favorite Biltmore Sprite for about 75 people. Pam and I wrote our own vows and the day was perfect. My brother, Tim, was my best man and Pam's sister, Paula, was the maid of honor. Ian and Riley were groomsmen along with Bill Macdonald, Tim Wallace, John Fallon, and Pam's brother Peter. We had a great band and danced the night away in the Aztec Room while trying to drink the Biltmore out of Veuve Cliquot. It was a perfect wedding. Rather than going on a honeymoon, Pam and I stayed for a few more days at the Biltmore and enjoyed more time with Ian and Riley including having another celebratory dinner at Flemings, our favorite steak restaurant in Phoenix.

In the meantime, we had moved out of the Boykin Hotel and not finding anything we wanted to rent or buy in town, I bought a house in the beautiful suburb of Russell, about half an hour from Cleveland. It was the most fabulous house I have ever owned, and the worst real estate deal I have ever made. We bought a fully furnished, 4,000 square foot house—closer to 6,000 if you count the fully renovated basement with bar and entertainment room... just what the two of us needed—called Blackstone Manor. It got that name because everything in the house was black and white. It was spectacular. The only problem was that the house was in Cleveland. The owner wanted $1 million for it, and I wound up paying $600,000. It also had a full workout room with a treadmill and a weight machine. It had a loft that Ian and Riley loved because it had a couch and big screen TV, so they could play video games and we all could have *Law and Order* marathons when they came to visit. I loved to drive so I would often drive about half an hour into town just to get a pizza that we would eat with a great bottle of wine on a Tuesday or Wednesday night. Collecting great wine became a little bit of a hobby for me. We found that we preferred to drink the wine rather than store it.

The house was also great because it was adjacent to a stable, so Pam could ride whenever she wanted, and she joined the local fox hunting club. At that time Pam started doing some work for Joyce Geiger, our friend from Affirmative, in setting up her web site and analytics database. Because we were hoping to stay in Ohio for a while—after making a large investment in the house—I joined Mayfield Country Club, outside of Cleveland to play golf.

One downside of our living in Ohio was that I was still a long way away from the boys. But Cleveland was a lot closer to New York than Dallas. I would occasionally make the seven hour drive from Cleveland to Montclair and back in a day, just for parent/teacher conferences.

But Cleveland was not to be. Late in 1999 Bob and I got into a serious argument over a deal I wanted us to do in Carmel, California. Bob didn't like the deal and the disagreement contributed to my prompt departure from Boykin on relatively good terms.

I wasn't sure exactly what we should do next, but both Pam and I thought that it was best to move back to New York. Since the wedding, we had been in regular contact with Bill and Kerry Graham and Kerry told Pam about an attractive position at the USGA (United States Golf Association) at its headquarters in Bedminster, New Jersey about an hour from NYC. I encouraged Pam to take the job, and she did. Living in Manhattan was not an option since it would have meant at least an hour drive each way for Pam, but I still needed to be close to midtown for whatever I was going to do. So we wound up renting a very nice two-bedroom apartment right on the water in Weehawken, New Jersey at a complex called Riva Pointe. The apartment had fantastic views. It worked out well for me, too, because I could be closer to the boys on weekends. Even though they came to visit us in both Dallas and Cleveland and spent a week with us in Phoenix every Christmas, it wasn't enough.

On the afternoon of Christmas Day, Pam and I would pick up the boys in Montclair and we would spend a week at the Villa in Arizona. On the plane to Phoenix I would devise trivia questions for the boys that they would have to answer to get clues to where I had hidden their presents around The Biltmore. I think both the boys and I enjoyed this very much. Our entire family would spend every New Year's Eve with Kerry and Bill Graham. Kerry and Bill were great with the boys. I always liked having Ian and Riley interacting with adults and encouraged them to do so. I also liked to make my time with the boys a fun learning experience. At very young ages they knew how to greet adults properly with a firm handshake and by always looking whoever they were meeting directly in the eye. I always thought that it was very important for the boys to learn how to be gentlemen and have proper manners. I would never hire (and would most always distrust) anyone who didn't look me in the eye when they met me. I also asked the boys to get in the habit of repeating the name of someone they were meeting when shaking hands to reinforce the memory of the person.

I don't remember how I met Bill Howell, but I will be forever grateful that I did. Bill's company, Boutique Hotel Group, had offices in the Empire State Building. While it was a pretty cool address, I didn't enjoy having to go through a metal detector to get to my office every day. Among other things, BHG managed three great boutique hotels in NYC: The Mansfield, on 44TH Street just West of 5TH Avenue, the Shoreham, on 55TH Street just West of Fifth Avenue, and the Roger Williams, on 31ST Street and Madison Avenue. Pam would often drive in from New Jersey after work and we would end the day together at the very cozy M Bar at the Mansfield.

Riva Pointe was right next to a Ruth's Chris Steak House which, basically, became our kitchen. Pam and I went there at least four times a week and we would often just sit at the bar and have a big salad and a glass of wine for dinner. I was there so often that they gave me a charge account, so I could pay my bill monthly. I would try to see the boys every weekend. In the golf season we would go to play golf and hang out at MGC. In the winter the boys would often stay with us. We had a favorite waiter at Ruth's Chris; his name was Lonnie and he was a great guy. The boys got to know him so well that he would challenge them to a race in the lobby of the office building adjacent to Ruth's Chris after dinner; it was so much fun to watch.

While working with Bill Howell I met Jay DiGuilio who also worked at BHG. Jay had a very successful career as a Senior Executive in the timeshare industry for Hilton and Marriott. His best and most recent project was the successful transformation of the historic Custom House in Boston to a timeshare for Marriott. BHG unsuccessfully tried to buy the hotels we were managing. Bill and Jay did not get along well, and I liked Jay immediately.

Jay and I left BHG in early 2003 and formed Boutique Club, with me as CEO and Jay as President. Our goal was to form a consulting company that would focus on hospitality consulting and transforming boutique and luxury hotels to fractional ownership. We took office space on Madison Avenue in midtown. Jay had three young sons and lived in Rye, not far from where I had grown up. Jay and I had a very successful partnership until my injury. We did great deals all through the United States and the Caribbean. Our most successful deal came through Jay and involved selling the Roger Williams Hotel in New York. While the Roger Williams was our most lucrative transaction, my favorite deal with Jay was the formation of Willow Club. I think Jay and I were ahead of our time with the concept, which was to provide a variety of first-class amenities to its members. To start, members would have access to a Sky Box at Madison Square Garden for sporting events and concerts, a yacht to cruise around Manhattan, access to a suite at three Midtown boutique hotels and dinner reservations at fabulous restaurants like Daniel and Le Cirque. We went to several Rangers games in the Sky Box and attended both a Jack Johnson concert and a Tom Petty concert in June of 2010 with family, friends, and clients. The principals at MSG even gave me a Henrik Lundqvist jersey, which I gave to my brother-in-law Peter, who was a hockey goalie in high school and is still a rabid Rangers fan.

Sadly, Boutique Club did not survive my injury and we have not closed a deal since that date. Jay was a great partner and friend, and he and I were always a great team. I am not sure that I would have done any better if Jay had been the one injured.

One of the most enjoyable things Jay and I did while we were at Boutique Club was participate in the annual Meet the Money conference in LA sponsored by my friend Jim Butler of Jeffer Mangels Butler & Mitchell. Jim is the smartest attorney I have ever known. Not only is he a very accomplished attorney, he is a truly masterful marketer. He has transformed the Meet the Money conference from a one-day event with a few sponsors to one of the most important events in the hospitality industry. It now spans three days and involves all aspects of the industry. The conference brings together companies and hospitality executives to network by participating in lectures and panel discussions. Jay and I were both speakers and moderators for many years and got a lot of business from our participation in the conferences. Jim always had a spectacular closing party at his home in Beverly Hills after the conference for one last opportunity to mingle in a more relaxed atmosphere. Pam and I became good friends with Jim and his significant other, Lana, and we would usually stay at the party after the crowd had left for a last glass of wine before we headed back to New York.

In July of 2003, I had one of the most incredible experiences of my life. My good friend, Bill Macdonald, invited me to Bohemian Grove. Bohemian Grove is a private men's club in the woods of northern California. The "Grove" has hosted several presidents, titans of industry, and famous musicians. The Grove is divided into several "camps," each of which has its own signature drink. There is great music everywhere and the men I got to meet and spend time with were some of the most powerful, influential, and recognizable people in the country from all fields including politics, business, and the arts. Despite the high-profile nature of the guests, no business is allowed to be conducted while at the Grove. In fact, guests are told that "weaving spiders come not here"—meaning that all business dealings are to be left outside the entrance to the Grove. Those who break that bond are politely asked to leave and never return. The whole event was about a large group of men just spending time meeting and talking to each other and listening to great music. All dining was in a large communal area with 20-foot benches. There were plays at night and lectures on various topics every day by the lake by some very famous people. It was truly one of the most special events of my life, I just wish I could really remember more of the specifics about the experience.

After I had spent a great weekend at the Grove, Pam picked me up at the front entrance in a green Jaguar convertible. It was the perfect car for the drive to Napa and Sonoma. We stayed at the Auberge du Soleil in Napa, one of my favorite hotels, and had a great time seeing our good friends, Tim and Patsy Wallace in Sonoma. We spent a few days visiting our favorite wineries for tastings and snacks and often ending our day with a final glass of wine at the Jack London Lodge in the Sonoma City square. It was great fun.

CHAPTER 10

On February 29, 2004, Pam's sister Pierrette married Sandeep Manchanda in Delhi, India. It was, and still is, my only trip to Asia. The wedding and the trip were incredible. In typical Indian fashion, the wedding lasted three days and there were hundreds of guests. Pam and Paula were both bridesmaids. On the wedding day, the sisters wore custom-made saris. The reception and the whole experience was very special. Pam and I also made it to the Taj Mahal, an incredible structure. As a real estate specialist, I often wonder how such a magnificent landmark could be constructed in 1632 and be in better condition than some 10-year-old buildings in New York City.

Pam and I thought that after traveling all the way to India, we should stop somewhere on the way back home for some more fun, so we chose Paris. I had never been to France and because we wanted to do something special we stayed about 30 minutes outside Paris in Versailles at the historic Trianon Palace. On our last night in Paris, the concierge at Trianon Palace arranged for us to have a fantastic dinner overlooking the Eiffel Tower. It was a very special trip.

Another amazing vacation trip for Pam and me was on September 30, 2006 when my good friend Bill Macdonald married the lovely Louisa Spring in Rome. Bill was a producer for the hit TV Series *Rome* at the time. I was an usher for Bill at the wedding and Ian and Riley also were there. We all, including the boys, wore kilts for the ceremony and were serenaded by a bagpiper walking to the reception. It was great fun and, as you might imagine, we (not the boys) drank our fair share of single malt scotch and great French Bordeaux. My favorite photograph from the wedding (and one of my all-time favorite photographs) is one of Ian, Riley and me walking away from the ceremony in our kilts. I had the photo framed and it hangs prominently in our house. Since it was very close to my 50TH birthday, Pam and I wanted to stay and explore Rome and celebrate my birthday with the boys. We did a little sightseeing and got to see the Colosseum and stayed at the Grand Hotel in Rome. The concierge at the Grand was terrific, he arranged for us to have a special tour of the Vatican which avoided the long lines of tourists and made reservations for us at the Mirabelle restaurant atop the 5-Star Hotel Splendid Royal overlooking St. Peter's Basilica with the Vatican in the distance. The view and experience were so spectacular that even Ian and Riley said "Wow."

As much as we liked our place at Riva Point, we were renting the apartment and the owner was coming back from a stint abroad. I found a great alternative in *The New York Times* in April of 2005. It was a special deal involving a four-bedroom house on five acres in Bedford, in Westchester County (with a pool and tennis court) for eight months of the year and a two-bedroom luxury, doorman apartment at Manhattan Place in Murray Hill in Manhattan for the other four months. Both homes were furnished, and the split was August to March in Bedford and April to July in NYC. Amazingly, the rent was not significantly more than we were currently paying. I made an appointment with the listing broker for both of us to see the Bedford house on Saturday morning. When Pam came home that night, I told her what I had found and said that if the house was still available on Saturday we were going to take it. We met the landlords, Jim and Joanne Cohen, who Pam and I liked right away. Jim was also a New York attorney and Joanne was a successful art dealer in New York. We also learned that Joanne, like Pam, was an avid rider and had a horse, named Topaz, that we also could rent as part of the deal.

The house was fantastic and was beautifully furnished and we signed the lease that morning. The stable was a short drive from the house which made Pam very happy.

By then, Pam had left the USGA and taken a job with a large commercial real estate firm in NYC with offices adjacent to Grand Central Station. When we lived in the Bedford house, Pam and I would pick up Jay in Rye every morning. Pam would take the train from Rye to Grand Central to avoid traffic and Jay and I would spend the remainder of the drive on the phone. In the evening we would often stop at Cipriani Dolce in the GC Concourse or the Campbell Apartments, a more intimate GC bar, for a very cold, very dry, Stoli martini. On the way home on Thursday and Friday, after dropping Jay off, Pam and I would often stop at Ruby's in Rye for dinner at the bar with our favorite bartender, Turner. Tim would often join us at Ruby's.

The only real restaurant in Bedford is The Bedford Post, a wonderful, very intimate but casual bistro with great food and service. Richard Gere is one of the owners. The Post became our kitchen on Saturday and Sunday, and we still try to go there whenever we are in the area. We saw Richard Gere regularly. One evening Richard was coming downstairs from the private dining room and tripped right in front of our table so Pam can now say that Richard Gere "fell for her."

My good friend from Montclair Golf Club, Dave DiBrigida, had joined a club in Bethlehem, Pennsylvania, where he went to school at Lehigh, called Saucon Valley and suggested that I join, too. Since I obviously love joining clubs, I did. I think that Saucon Valley is the finest private golf course facility in the country. It has three spectacular championship golf courses, great dining facilities and guest cottages on the grounds for overnight stays. When Pam and I were on the New York leg of our Bedford rental we often would spend our weekends at Saucon Valley playing with Dave and staying in the cottages. Saucon Valley has hosted several PGA and LPGA events, perhaps the most significant being the U.S. Women's Open in July of 2009. Saucon Valley also will host the USGA Senior Championship tournament in 2022.

When we were living in Bedford, Pam didn't always join me for golf. I would often go to play golf with Dave on Saturdays at Saucon Valley, so we needed a second car so that Pam would not be stranded while I was gone. I found a great deal in *The New York Times* on a used cherry red Porsche 911 Turbo. Both Pam and I had learned how to drive a standard shift car when we were young—both of our first cars were MGs—Pam an MGB and me an MG Midget, which is basically two motorcycles strung together. We both loved the Porsche, but it was really Pam's car and she looked great driving around Bedford, to the Bedford Post with me for brunch on Sunday and to the stables to take Topaz out for a jaunt around the Bedford Riding Lanes.

Also, during our New York stint, we started going to Shun Lee and Sparks. In my opinion, Shun Lee is the best Chinese restaurant in New York and Sparks is the best steakhouse. Both also were great for entertaining clients, which I did often because I was always treated like a celebrity (I'm sure my reputation as a good tipper helped). We still go to Shun Lee whenever we are in New York and I still get the royal "Mr. Murphy" treatment. Pam is convinced that my injury was partially caused by eating too much red meat and drinking too many large Stoli martinis, so we don't go to Sparks much anymore. I also attribute my injury to my inexplicable resistance to exercise and being terribly overweight. In 2011 the host at Sparks was so gracious that he gave me an enlarged page from their menu that I gave to Ian as a gift, because the boys loved to go there with us.

CHAPTER 11

Ian graduated with honors from Montclair High School in June of 2007 and was accepted to Williams for college early decision, which made me very happy and very proud. I thought it was appropriate to do something grand to celebrate his accomplishment, so I arranged a vacation trip to Ireland for Pam, Ian, and Riley. We had an amazing time, staying at Adare Manor for three nights in Limerick and The K Club for three nights in Straffan. Adare Manor is a 5-Star Resort in a castle and an architectural masterpiece with a Tom Fazio-designed golf course and The K Club is a more modern 5-Star Resort with two fantastic golf courses, one of which was home to the 2006 Ryder Cup. Since the boys were new to golf and the rough on a links course is very punishing, we went through a lot of golf balls every day—but had a fantastic trip. The saying is, "If you don't like the weather in Ireland… wait an hour." We often had torrential rain and bright sunshine in the same day. I think the most fun Pam and the boys had was when we went to the local pubs in Doneraile and Cork, where my parents were from. The Irish love telling stories and they love Irish Americans, so several of the older patrons would try to convince, especially me, that they knew my parents, regaling us with fantastic stories. It was great fun and I think I even let the boys have a pint of Guinness.

We had so much fun on the Ireland trip for Ian that we decided to do it again when Riley graduated from Montclair High School in June of 2010 to celebrate his admission to the University of Pennsylvania. We spent most of the vacation at The K Club and also stayed a couple of nights at the Ritz Carlton in Powerscourt.

We often went into town after golf to visit the local pubs. The boys by then were old enough to enjoy a pint of Guinness with us. Of the two golf courses at The K Club, our favorite was the one named for the famed Arnold Palmer, who also loved The K Club. The boys, both being very good athletes, played much better golf this time which made the experience even more fun. We often would end the day in the fabled Vintage Crop Cocktail Bar which has amazing equestrian art that Pam especially loved. The owner of The K Club, Michael Smurfit, is an avid equestrian and Vintage Crop is the name of his prized gelding which was the first Irish horse to surpass 1 million pounds in winnings as well as winning the Melbourne Cup in 1993. Both times we were at The K Club, the man behind the bar was the magnificent Remy who always poured a perfect pint of Guinness. To our surprise and delight, Remy still remembered Pam and me when we went back to Ireland for my 60TH birthday in 2016.

While Ian was a good lacrosse player playing defense at Montclair, Riley was a great lacrosse player at Montclair and played midfield. I tried to go to as many games as possible during all four years and Pam and I spent a lot of time with Riley driving to Baltimore, the biggest Northeast city for lacrosse tournaments. I loved it and Riley had a very tight team who were all good friends. Whenever I got to drive to a game with Riley (and often his teammates) I made them listen to some of my favorite books on Sherlock Holmes and Hercule Poirot. I figured it was a good learning experience and the boys even seemed to like it. Riley's team won the State Championship in his senior year, 2010, and Riley played a great game. It was a stellar conclusion to four great years at Montclair for Riley and his teammates. Riley was recruited by several colleges with top lacrosse teams and decided to go to the University of Pennsylvania, an Ivy League school in Philadelphia, once again making me a very proud father.

Pam and I loved to go to Williamstown in the summer to play golf at Taconic and eat at our favorite restaurants. Williamstown and Taconic are beautiful in the summer and we would go as often as possible. One of our favorite events was the Red White and Blue tournament held at Taconic on July 4TH every year. It was a partner tournament and we always played with our good friends Peter and Joan Zegas. Peter had retired from a successful career as an executive in the cosmetics industry and Joan did advertising consulting work for several major companies. Joan is petite, like Pam and is a great golfer and competitor. Neither the team of Joan and Pam nor Peter and I ever won the tournament, but we did place occasionally and, as Joan liked to say, "won the socks."

I sold the Villa at the Biltmore in Arizona in 2008 to my good friend Bill Imperato. Pam and I continued the tradition of picking up Ian and Riley on Christmas Day for a holiday trip. Instead of going to Phoenix, my good friend Scott Silver invited us to stay at his home in Wellington, Florida. Scott is a successful real estate executive, and he and I had done several deals together. Scott and Laura had a beautiful home in a gated community known as Versailles and we had a great time there. Pam loved it because Versailles is in Wellington, home of the International Polo Club. It was also close to the Breakers Hotel in Palm Beach and Pam and I celebrated several New Year's Eve dinners there after the boys headed back home to spend New Year's Eve with their friends.

All throughout 2010, I was doing a lot of business in the Caribbean. It looked like that was going to continue to be a focus for our hotel company. In the fall of 2010 we were visiting the Silvers when I saw a house for sale in Versailles that I thought would be perfect for us. The price was good, and Pam purchased it in November of 2010. We had gotten to know and like the area and the community so well by then... and it was a perfect place from which to travel to the Caribbean. The house was a ranch style, three bedrooms, three and a half baths, that had a gourmet kitchen and a vaulted ceiling in the living room. The community also had a health club that I should have used more often than I did. Since we had moved back to an apartment in New York and did not need two cars in the city, we sent the Porsche to Wellington and left it there as our "Florida car." I had also heard about the Wanderers Golf Club in Wellington. The Wanderers Club had a fantastic championship 18-hole track. Prior to joining, we were asked to play a round with the head golf professional at the club. We had a great time and were very impressed with the course and the club. After the round we asked what we needed to do to join. Our playing partner said, "You're in. I am the application committee."

We went down to Florida often during 2010 and always enjoyed it. We found out that the golf professional of the Wanderers Club was also very involved in The International Polo Club. We loved to play golf at the Wanderers Club and attend Polo matches when the players were in Wellington. The Polo Club had a spectacular Sunday brunch. The Clubhouse at the Wanderers Club was beautiful, with an equestrian theme and two original Remington bronze statues in the entrance. I liked them so much that I bought two replica Remingtons for our house. The Porsche was a perfect Florida car and always got us a good parking space at the club and at Polo matches. Pam often drove since a beautiful woman will always get a better reception than an overweight, balding guy when driving a red Porsche. Pam loves Polo like I love golf and we both equally loved to go to Polo matches. Pam loved to watch the talented riders, I loved it mostly because the matches were always sponsored by Veuve Clicquot and after the third chukka there was usually a truck on the field pouring glasses of free champagne. Also, the ceremony of "stomping the divots" at halftime was fun.

In the summer of 2011, Pam got a call from her good friend Luciana who told her that she had rented a beautiful three-bedroom house in Tuscany, Italy for a week and that one of the couples that was planning to go had to cancel. She asked: Would we like to go? It took Pam about 10 seconds to say Yes. The house was in Lucca and was unbelievable with three full bedrooms and a pool. I don't remember much else about the trip except that the house was up on a cliff and the only way to town was a one-lane road so I (and anyone driving) had to honk at each bend to avoid a collision. I'm sure we had an amazing time visiting several wineries in Tuscany. The funniest story Pam tells about the trip is my driving into town one afternoon and I was lost, which I know is true because even though I often did the driving for us, and we have driven a lot, I have always had, even before my injury, a terrible sense of direction. I'm not sure how I ever got from Cleveland to New Jersey or New York to Florida—never mind getting around in European countries driving without a navigation system but somehow, I did. While I was driving us one lovely afternoon in Tuscany I was pulled over by a young carabinieri because I had apparently crossed over a line in the road while trying to get to a parking spot. I'm sure he thought I was just another stupid American tourist. He let me go, but said to me very clearly "you see-a da line—don-a cross-a da line" and shook his finger at me. Pam probably could have helped me because she still speaks passable Italian, but she was having too much fun watching me get scolded. Pam uses that line on me now when I do something stupid, which is often. "You see-a da line—don-a cross-a da line" and shakes her finger at me.

CHAPTER 12

The attendant in the Delta Lounge found my Blackberry phone and smartly called the last number I had called, which was Pam's. He told her what had happened to me and that I was being rushed by ambulance to Jamaica Plain Hospital in Queens. He couldn't tell her if I was alive or dead. I can't imagine what she went through. Pam first called her sister Paula and didn't get her right away and then called my brother Tim. Pam did get to Pierrette who called Uncle Tom Elmquist (Barbara's brother), who is a well-known cardiologist in NYC, who, after some wrangling, had me transferred that night to New York Presbyterian Columbia Medical Center on West 158TH Street in Manhattan. Pam's father, who was a neurosurgeon (and passed away way too young), always told her that if you are ever hospitalized, make sure you are taken to Columbia Presbyterian. I was admitted to the neurological intensive care unit and was diagnosed with cardiac arrest and a traumatic anoxic brain injury. Tim called Ian, Riley, Peggy and Billy Mac. They all came to the Hospital as soon as they could. Ian had to come from Williams and Riley from Penn. Billy arrived from Los Angeles, he had jumped on a flight immediately after hearing the news, and had not even changed clothes. Billy was so upset at the situation that he smashed a glass table and had cuts all over his hand. Pam sent him to our apartment, so he could shower and change clothes.

I was unconscious for five days. The paramedics had broken my ribs to get to my heart, the only bones I have ever broken except my clavicle in grammar school playing football. The doctors also had to perform a tracheotomy so I could breathe and had to drill into my brain to place monitors that checked for seizures. I was also on a ventilator and had pneumonia from the hypothermia treatment. I was a mess, but alive. Pam said it looked like I had about a hundred wires coming out of every part of my body. Billy stayed almost a week and Tim, Siobhan, Ian, Riley and Peggy came to visit every day. I'm sure the boys would have stayed longer but they had to get back to school. Despite our differences, Peggy has become a good friend since my injury, something I'm very happy about. We talk often about the boys and Pam and I have had a lot of fun with her and her new husband Gregg whenever we get together at one of the boy's events. She is truly a great person, a fantastic mother, and I am forever grateful that she came to the hospital for me.

Billy said that Ian was incredible with the doctors and the entire Pillone family were amazing. To that end, Paula, a nurse practitioner and former Assistant Professor at Columbia University School of Nursing, seemed to know everyone at the hospital and she made sure that I had the "Mercedes" of beds.

I opened my eyes after five days, but I still couldn't speak or really recognize anyone or anything. I was completely dazed by all the pain killing drugs and I was still on a ventilator. Pam says that I did start to smile, and I seemed to respond positively to Billy's very deep voice. The doctors kept waiting for me to 'follow commands' as a sign that I was coming to. Pam told them that I've never 'followed commands' in the past so it is going to be a while. I remained in intensive care for two weeks and then was in the stepdown unit at Columbia for another two weeks.

I had started to speak somewhat weakly and had started to get a little cognitive recognition back during the second week. The fact that I could recognize Pam was a big step for me and for her. Just before my discharge from the intensive care step down unit I was able to fully breath on my own so, thankfully, they removed the ventilator. Next was acute rehabilitation and I was transferred to NYU Medical Center on East 38TH Street on November 1ST which was a lot closer to our apartment on 1ST Avenue and much easier for Pam. Pam came in that first morning and started to cry. I asked her why and she told me that a doctor had told her that I would probably never walk again and that I'd probably only be able to hold my grandchildren on my lap in my wheelchair at family gatherings. I guess she was trying to be positive by saying that I was going to live long enough to see my grandchildren. I told Pam that was not going to happen, and I promised her that I would be walking by Christmas.

The next morning when my nurse came into my room, I was not in my bed. That must have really freaked the nurse out, I had gotten out of bed and "walked" to the bathroom but was too weak and collapsed on the floor. So the nurses put up gates around my bed and strapped me in. The only way for me to get out of bed was to be hoisted in the air with straps, guided by two attendants, and then gently set down in a wheel chair. Something had to change. I didn't enjoy being "punished" for trying to walk. I asked my physical therapist to push me as much as possible, so I could try to recover as quickly as possible. I had some physical, some speech and some occupational therapy every day. The occupational therapy was more to help me challenge, and hopefully, stimulate my cognitive functioning and teach me simple things that I didn't even know how to do like brush my teeth or write, certainly not to prepare me for a job.

I had some great hallucinations when I was at NYU. Pam's favorite was that I was in a hotel and not a hospital, which is understandable since I had spent most of my career in the hospitality industry. I would get upset when Pam said she had to leave for the night. I said that all the other wives were staying with their husbands in their hotel rooms. After Pam had been with me for a few hours, I also would tell her to go to the hotel bar and get a glass of wine to relax for a while. I also had a recurring hallucination that I was in a great Italian restaurant and in a hotel next to a golf course. At least I was having fun.

The most fun night I had at NYU was when Jay, Devin Wakeford, who worked for us, and Scott Silver came to visit me. Pam had given me the game *Trivial Pursuit*, which I loved and used to be very good at, to try to play during my waking hours and stimulate my brain. I hated being in my room all day and would always take dinner opposite from the large nurse's station. That night I brought the game to dinner and we played with the nurses for hours. Devin is model handsome and a tennis pro which probably was a reason for the nurses letting us have so much fun for so long. When I left NYU one of the nurses told me that it was the most fun she had ever had at work.

On November 29TH I was transferred to the sub-acute facility at Kateri Residences on the Upper West Side on Riverside Drive and 88TH Street. When I arrived at Kateri, I once again took the liberty of "walking" to the bathroom and this time, I actually made it. The next day the nurses gave me a walker, which I hated, but I much preferred it to a wheelchair. I spent as much time as I could every day walking up and down the halls on my floor with my walker and a nurse. My legs, of course, were still very weak after spending almost two months being mostly bed ridden.

Our lease was ending at Manhattan Place so, in addition to having to go to work and worry about me every day, Pam had to find a new apartment for us quickly. Thankfully she found a very large one-bedroom apartment, in a doorman building on 3RD Avenue and 68TH Street—a little closer to Kateri. I continued to take speech, physical and occupational therapy every day and Pam came to visit me every day which greatly helped my mood and attitude.

The first time I saw our new apartment was on December 10TH and it was great. Pam and I were going to Luciana's 50TH birthday party. Luci had arranged a fantastic dinner party for about 30 people at the renowned Bouley Test Kitchen on West 21ST Street, just West of Fifth Avenue in the Flatiron District of NYC with a tasting menu and wine pairings. It was great that Ian was in town with his girlfriend and he helped me get into my suit and tie, my first real clothes in two months. I felt so wonderful. I did have to wear sneakers and, even though I had been using a walker, I also had to take a wheelchair by hospital rules. Pam recalls that the dinner was fantastic and that I was able to converse with people in a fairly coherent way. David Bouley himself even came out from the kitchen and shook my hand.

I had started walking down the halls of Kateri holding the walker aloft, so I knew I had to get out of the hospital soon to maintain my sanity and my progress.

I was able to leave Kateri on December 23RD and Paula, Peter and Amanda, his girlfriend, all came to our apartment to greet me home. I had spent a total of 78 days in four hospitals and it was so awesome for me to be home. Looking back, I now know that the care I got throughout all that time had been exceptional, as was the support from Pam and both her family and my family. As I was leaving Kateri with Pam my favorite nurse came up to me and hugged me. She said that she had underestimated my tenacity and said that my unwavering positive attitude was my "ace in the hole." I told her how much I appreciated her thoughts and told her that it was mostly the love from Pam that made the difference in my recovery.

The next evening, Christmas Eve, as was our family tradition, Pam and I and the Pillone family went to Uncle Tom's fabulous apartment on the Upper West Side for Christmas Eve dinner. Uncle Tom and his great wife, Peggy always hosted an amazing dinner party for about 30 people. As I had promised Pam at NYU, I walked on my own power into Uncle Tom's apartment. Pam and I both cried as we hugged, and all the guests at the party gave me a standing ovation. Pam had been with me every one of those 78 days. She was and is incredible and the main reason why I have had such a powerful and successful rehabilitation. I can't imagine what she had gone through. Walking into Uncle Tom's was a defining moment for me, but I told Pam that it was just the beginning of my recovery. A fun tradition at Uncle Tom's Christmas party is the reading by each guest of a line from Clement Moore's *A Visit from St. Nicholas* between dinner and dessert. I did get to participate, and Pam said that my lines were slurred but understandable. It was a perfect way to end my time in hospitals.

The fun continued the next day when I got to have Christmas breakfast with Pam, Tim, Siobhan and Bryeanna, Peter and Amanda at our apartment. We had my favorite, everything bagel with cream cheese and tomato. It was great to eat real food again. Pam said that Tim was awesome during the entire time I spent in all the hospitals. We went from breakfast to our traditional Christmas Day party at Lisa and Eric's house in New Jersey where everyone was very happy to see me out of the hospital and walking. It was another great day.

Paula and my friend Alan had started dating after they met at Columbia and were living together in an apartment on the Upper West Side. Pam and I spent New Year's Eve 2011 with them in their apartment where, if we leaned out the window we could see the Tiffany ball drop in Times Square at midnight. We had a great time and Pam even let me have a sip of Veuve Clicquot as the ball dropped. It was an awesome way to start the new year.

On January 5, 2012 the New York Giants and Eli Manning shocked the world and all the bookies by beating the New England Patriots in the Super Bowl 21-17. Pam and I were with Tim and Siobhan at the Larchmont Yacht Club. It was a great way to start 2012. Normally I would have had a few Montesano Coolers, the signature drink of LYC made with Mount Gay Rum but instead I had a few non-alcoholic beers while the others enjoyed the Coolers. I was just so happy to be at the Club with my family.

CHAPTER 13

When I entered Columbia Presbyterian on October 7, 2011 I weighed 205 pounds, I was very overweight and unhealthy. When I left Kateri I weighed 185 pounds and I promised Pam that I would never be over 185 again. I now weigh 170 and, despite my TBI, am probably in the best physical shape I have been in since I was about 30 years old. I do some type of cardio exercise every day, when I'm home, no exceptions. During the day it's at least 40 minutes on the elliptical machine or spin bike and when I do the elliptical it's another 20 minutes of walking to and from our gym. On weekends Pam and I walk while we play golf; I use a pull cart and Pam usually carries her own bag. That's about seven miles of walking each day. Whenever we travel I will spend either an hour in the hotel gym or at least 45 minutes walking. Pam is in fantastic physical condition and also works out every day. She makes sure that I keep up with my exercising.

I had a day nurse for about six weeks after my release from Kateri on December 23, 2011 so that Pam could get to work, where she was a Senior Vice President for a major real estate company, and I could get to therapy, which I started early in 2012 at NYU Langone on 38TH Street and 1ST Avenue. NYU was exactly 30 blocks, exactly a mile and a half, and a direct shot from my apartment on 68TH Street. My nurse and I would walk to my therapy twice a week. Once I had started walking I was determined to get my speed back and would walk as fast as I could. When I started therapy it took me about 45 minutes in each direction. By the time we left New York in the summer of 2014 I could do it in 35 minutes. I had the same three therapies I had in my various hospitals. For the first few months after my release from Kateri, walking was the only exercise I could do. I asked my physical therapist to focus on trying to get some strength back into my legs, although the walking helped, but my balance was terrible. I asked my occupational therapist to try to challenge me with logic games and puzzles to try to get my brain working again. My speech therapist was the most challenged as it appears that the left frontal lobe of the brain, which controls speech was most affected by my injury. Even after extensive therapy and my own work at home I still have some aphasia today.

In the early morning of February, 2012, Amanda, Peter's girlfriend, was hit by a car while running at home in St. Simons Island in Georgia and was seriously injured. It was almost unbelievable that another member of the family was struck by a devastating injury so close to mine. She had years of the same type of therapy ahead of her that I went through. It was a devastating blow and Peter was Amanda's rock just as Pam had been for me after my injury. Amanda also has recovered remarkably well.

In early February, 2012, I told Pam that I didn't need my nurse anymore. She said that if my occupational therapist approved it would be alright. For two days I was able to walk with my therapist to my apartment and back without help and she approved the switch. It had become a fairly easy trip for me. My speech therapist told me that singing might help. I couldn't put Pam through the pain of my singing at home, so I would sing as I walked to and from therapy while trying to count the number of people who I passed. I don't think that the count was ever less than 700 and no one complained about my singing although I'm sure some thought I was crazy—which I am.

Pam and I went to Mass every month starting in the spring of 2012. I had gone from going to Mass every day in grade school to about once a month at Andover and Williams to twice a year

(Easter and Christmas) once I got to New York. Knowing that the Good Lord had saved me, Pam and I had prayed often together when I was in the hospital and I thought I should let Him know that I was grateful and wanted to come back in the fold. We went to St. Vincent Ferrer Church in New York on 67TH Street and Lexington Avenue, very close to our apartment. It is a very nice Church with beautiful Gothic Revival architecture. There was a Starbucks very close to the Church, so Pam and I would go afterwards for cappuccino and breakfast.

Although she still looked like she was 40 years old, Pam's sister, Paula turned 50 on April 17TH, 2012. To celebrate, the family went to the 5-Star Resort in Sea Island, Georgia, The Cloister, because Peter and Amanda, who were living next door in St. Simons Island, had access to a friends and family rate. The Cloister is an amazing resort. Pam's birthday is a day before Paula's, so we had Pam's birthday dinner in the Georgian Room at The Cloister, the only 5-Star restaurant in Georgia and it was fantastic. Pam again let me have a glass of Champagne to celebrate. We celebrated Paula's birthday the next night at a great seafood restaurant while sitting outside next to the water. Among its many terrific amenities, The Cloister has an amazing golf facility and Pam arranged for us to have a group golf lesson. I was terrible. To be good at golf requires good balance, good eye-hand coordination and the ability to have a singular focus. I had none of those things, but I tried. The facility had a state of the art video mechanism and big screen for teaching, so I got to see how poorly I did. It was a waste of great equipment, but I was very glad that I had the lesson and I tried to learn from it. It made me more determined to get better. I liked golf too much to give it up.

I wanted to do something to try to continue to improve my balance and eye-hand coordination, so I signed up for tennis lessons at the Sutton Place Tennis facility on 60TH Street and 1ST

Avenue. It was one day a week for eight weeks. It was also a good way to break up my week and get some exercise. I was always just a fair tennis player, but this was fun. It helped both my physical and mental focus and playing in competition was something that I liked. I wasn't great but by the end of the sessions, I could keep up with my fellow players which I viewed as progress. I also started bouncing a tennis ball at home for about five minutes every day with each hand to help with my hand eye coordination. After a few months I got up to 40 repetitions.

Pam and I wanted to get out of NY during summer weekends. Our favorite places were Luci's house in East Hampton and Williamstown. Luci had a fabulous four-bedroom house and we loved to stop in for dinner at Citta Nuova, which had great Italian food and a great outdoor patio, when we arrived late on a Friday night. Luci and Pam introduced me to "spinning" that summer. Spinning is stationary cycling in a competitive class environment with an instructor and music. I liked it right away. It's a tremendous cardio workout for about 45 minutes. Pam is very good. I was awful at first and Luci is a professional and the fastest "spinner" I have ever seen. The class also involves standing on the bike for part of the time (second position) and using light weights for some arm exercises. At the beginning of the summer I had to stay seated and didn't even try the weights. By the end of the summer I could do both and was very happy with my progress. Spinning also requires special shoes that allow you to lock into the pedals for stability. At first, I needed help from Pam to "lock in" and I had no chance of getting the shoes out of the pedals. I guess my ankles were just not strong enough yet. By the end of the summer I could do both by myself.

We also loved to go to Williamstown whenever we could. We would always stop at the Bedford Post for breakfast on the way for a little reminiscing and since they had a great frittata on the menu. We often played golf at Taconic with our good friends Peter and Joan Zegras. Before my injury, Peter and I and Joan and Pam would play as partners in the annual "Red, White and Blue" tournament on The Fourth of July. Peter is a mid-handicap golfer and Joan is a Club Champion. Early in the summer they were very accommodating and allowed me to tee up every shot and pick up my ball whenever necessary, which was often. I took a lesson from the legendary Rick Pohle, who had been the golf professional at Taconic since 1983, but it was too soon. While I was walking reasonably well I still had a long way to go on balance and hand-eye coordination. I was frustrated but by the end of the summer, I could get the ball around the course for nine holes.

One summer weekend afternoon while we were getting coffee after golf at Tunnel City in Williamstown, Pam got a call from her sister, Pierrette, that she had just been diagnosed with breast cancer. It was devastating. There had been three major medical crises in our family in less than a year. We went back to NY immediately and to Pierrette's home in Westchester, NY. Pam and I tried to see Pierrette most Sundays and help her and her husband Sandeep with their three young children. Her sister Paula was also there to help all the time. Pierrette went through chemotherapy for several weeks and had surgery in Texas. She has made a full recovery and is now (amazingly) running marathons again.

CHAPTER 14

My brother Tim was renting a house in Myrtle Beach during St. Patrick's Day 2013 and invited me to join him for a few days of golf and fun. Although I had flown twice in 2012 with Pam, she was very concerned about my flying alone. I told her that it would be a good test for me to do it by myself. She relented but wanted me to wear an "I have a defribulator" sticker on my shirt when going through security. Of course, I said no to that idea. Since I was flying Spirit Airlines and only going for two nights, I put everything I needed in my backpack, which I had always used as a briefcase before my injury. The flight going both ways was fine, and I didn't set off any metal alarms at the security checkpoints, which was Pam's main worry. I had a great time with Tim who gave me a dozen ProV1 golf balls, the best balls on the market. I'm sure that I lost most of them during our two days of golf, but I did play a lot better than I had the previous summer. I really felt like I was "playing" golf for the first time since my injury, even though I was still terrible. We found a decent restaurant for corned beef and cabbage. Tim let me have a pint of Guinness and we enjoyed St. Patrick's Day. It was a very good trip for me and I was proud of myself for being able to travel alone. Pam also was very happy and impressed. Also, I really enjoyed spending a few days with Tim. Tim has become my best friend and, except for Pam, my biggest supporter since my injury. He and I talk on the phone at least three times a week and it's great for me.

In early June of 2013 Pam and I went to Williamstown for my 35TH Williams reunion. We had a great time. On Saturday afternoon,

Farmer, RJ, the Vommer and I went with our wives to see the new Aquatic Facility now dedicated to the Sammer. It was incredible, like something you would see at UCLA. The Sammer and his wife were there to show us around. The Pool had a couple of huge walls of fame showing the history of all-time Williams records for the various events. I think both Farmer and Vommer were still on it. That's how good they were. That night we danced the night away. My roommate Frank Carr was the DJ and master of ceremonies and Farmer was elected President of our Class. I got to see a lot of my classmates, most of whom didn't know about my injury, but they were wonderfully supportive and thought that I had made a lot of progress in a year and a half. There was a moment of silence for a classmate who had recently passed away and though I don't remember it, Pam told me that it gave her chills and she almost started to cry thinking about how close I had come to dying.

That Thanksgiving we went to Fort Lauderdale, as we had many times. An annual tradition for the family at Thanksgiving in Fort Lauderdale is to participate in the "Turkey Trot." The Turkey Trot is a 5K (3.2 miles) running race that takes place on Highway A1A. It started in 2011 with a few hundred participants and now it has a few thousand. I wanted to participate but had to walk. Pam put away her competitive nature and walked with me. I told her that I would be running the following year.

After graduating Cum Laude from Williams, which is an incredible achievement, Ian decided that his best path was in medicine and started studying for the MCAT exam in early 2013. Riley is incredibly smart, in a manner similar to me, but I think that Ian is brilliant. He has an incredible work ethic and an equally incredible ability to focus while studying very complex and challenging subjects. He said that the studying was miserable, and the exam was very difficult, but he, of course, aced it. Ian, Riley and, even I, were always good exam takers. Ian interviewed at the best Medical Schools in the country—Harvard, Yale, UVA and Denver but decided on Tufts University in Boston. He said that he felt that there was something special about his interviews and the students and doctors he met there.

Pam needed to travel for work and I assured her that I would be alright by myself for two nights, the maximum that Pam would travel for. I was already making my own breakfast and making my own arrangements to get to my therapy appointments. Pam had taught me how to use my computer again and I put every appointment and important dates in my calendar and I promised her that I wouldn't use the stove. Everything was in easy walking distance from our apartment if I needed anything and since every restaurant delivers in NYC I could just order pizza or Shun Lee for dinner. We still rarely cooked, but now we ordered in a lot for dinner rather than going out every night. Sunday was Shun Lee night, which we both loved. Also, since we didn't have any hard liquor in the apartment, I couldn't raid the liquor cabinet. I also became a fan of Post-it® notes and would leave myself reminders for almost everything. I still do that today. Pam's trip was fine, and I didn't burn down the apartment.

That Thanksgiving, I ran by myself in the Turkey Trot in Florida. It took me just over 50 minutes, which is about 16 minutes per mile. That's not much faster than a quick walk but it gave me a standard to go by and a goal to beat for next year.

On April 16, 2014 we celebrated Pam's 50TH birthday. Like all women, she was not happy about being 50, but I assured her that she looked even more beautiful now than she did at our wedding almost 15 years before. Pam's mother, Barbara's significant other, Adam Sandford, owns a spectacular home in Rancho Leonero, near Los Cabos, Mexico. Adam was an immensely successful Engineer who had developed several patents for medical devices. His house was right on the beach with an awesome view of The

Sea of Cortez. He invited us to spend Pam's 50TH there. Adam had been a competitive deep-sea fisherman for many years and had known Pam and the Pillones for almost 40 years. Rancho Leonero is known for its awesome fishing and many seasoned sport fishermen stay at the resort by the same name. The resort is a very short walk from Adam's house where we went for breakfast every morning and for one cerveza every afternoon. The bar at Rancho Leonero did not have non-alcoholic beer so Pam let me have one Pacifico Light, which is almost the same thing. The house was rustically stunning, and Pam and I got to stay in the beautiful separate Casita which is part of the house. Pam has always been in incredible shape and into exercising every day and wanted to help me recover as quickly as possible. We ran on the beach every morning before breakfast and kayaked in the afternoon. We ran for 40 minutes, which was about 4 miles for Pam and just under three miles for me. I was determined to beat my time in the 2013 Turkey Trot and running on sand was great practice. We had Pam's birthday celebration at a lunch at Palmilla, a 5-Star, One and Only resort. The whole experience was fantastic and the next day Pam and I played the golf course at Palmilla, which was stunning with spectacular vistas at every hole. I was starting to "play" golf again although I doubt that I broke 100. We also went deep sea fishing and Pam caught her first blue marlin. Despite growing up in a sport fishing family, blue marlin had eluded her. Adam was a terrific host and Pam said it was a very memorable birthday and it was another milestone for me having travelled abroad for the first time since my injury.

CHAPTER 15

Pam and I went to almost all of Riley's lacrosse games while he was at Penn and had a blast with the other parents while traveling to Penn and the other Ivy League schools. Riley had a great team with great teammates. Penn was having a career season in 2014 and we loved watching the games and cheering in the stands with the other parents. The Ivy League Championship was held on May 2ND and May 4TH at Harvard Stadium in Boston. Penn was ranked No. 3 in the tournament and was playing No. 2 ranked Cornell in the first game. It was a great game and Penn won in an upset 11-10. Harvard beat Yale 10-9 on the same day. The final was on May 4TH and Penn won in even a more stunning upset 7-5. The Penn defense was incredible and Brian Feeney, the goalie for Penn was spectacular and won MVP for the tournament. I was so happy for Riley.

Shortly after Penn's big win, Riley told me that his true passion was acting. Riley is very handsome, has a nearly photographic memory, making the recall of scripts easy for him, and, like me, was never nervous when speaking before an audience. He had become seriously interested in acting during his Junior Year at Penn. He expressed an interest in spending a summer in LA to get a better feel for the movie business to see whether acting was the right career move for him. Peggy wasn't thrilled with the idea at first, but eventually relented. I knew that the only way for him to be happy was to allow him to follow his passion. I called my friend Billy Macdonald in Hollywood and asked whether he could help Riley. He said of course, and Riley moved in with Billy and his wife Louisa that Summer. Billy's house had a separate detached apartment that he invited Riley to use. During that year Riley was cast in a movie, Hansel vs. Gretel. Though it was a B horror movie, it was an amazing experience for him. I was incredibly proud that he had been cast in a Hollywood movie that actually got produced. And I was especially thankful to Billy and Louisa for helping Riley. On the first day he arrived in LA I sent Riley a text with the words "Be Great" and one of the first things I have done every morning since then is send him a short encouraging text message. He said that he likes to know that I'm supporting him every day. I let him know not only that I love doing that, but that it's another cognitive exercise for me every day.

Earlier in 2014, Pam had taken on a new career role at her company and since there was no longer a need for her to be in NYC, asked her chief executive if she could move to Palm Beach and work from the office there. This made a lot of sense since Pam owned a home there. The counter offer was for Pam to lead a team in Boston for 15 months and that after that time she could probably move somewhere else. We thought that this could be great because Ian was in Boston for Medical School at Tufts and we could spend some time with him. We were busy looking for apartments in Boston during Riley's Ivy League lacrosse championship tournament at Harvard Stadium. We knew that we didn't need to buy anything or maintain anything large for 15 months and started looking for a two-bedroom apartment in town close to Pam's office. We didn't find anything we liked enough to rent for several weeks. Then I saw an ad in *The Boston Globe* for a brand-new luxury rental building in the Financial District, near Chinatown. The ad was offering a month's free rent for signing a lease and another month of free rent for attending a cocktail party showing. This sounded like our kind of deal, so we went to the party. The building was awesome, a full-service doorman building, the décor was modern and elegant, and the health club was fantastic.

We liked two apartments right away. The one I liked first had a fabulous curved window in the living room but only had 1 bedroom and very limited closet space which would never work. Pam just laughed at me for even suggesting that we could live there. We rented the apartment that Pam liked best, it was a large two-bedroom with great views, good closet space and on the same floor as the health club.

Because our new apartment was on the same floor as the health club, I had no excuse not to work out every day. The equipment in the health club was also brand new with state of the art elliptical machines, treadmills and other exercise machines. My favorite part of the health club was the 1000 square foot workout room with a 200-inch video screen that allowed you to take spinning classes since there were also 6 spin bikes. There were various video spin classes, but my favorite was the 52 Minute "Tour of Ireland". The class was difficult and took you on a trip all around Ireland. I loved it and got a lot better at spinning. I would normally spin every third day and do the elliptical machine and weight machines on the other days.

As we were leaving NY, I asked my occupational therapist if she had any recommendations for therapy hospitals in Boston. She suggested that I investigate the Spaulding Rehabilitation Center. I learned that it was the teaching hospital for the Harvard Medical School Department of Physical Medicine and Rehabilitation and the hospital that was most endorsed by professional athletes needing rehabilitation. I asked my NY doctor to arrange a transfer and he did. Spaulding is an awesome facility and my therapists were great. I had occupational, speech and physical therapy once again twice every week. I had a notebook for the homework I would get from each session. One of the challenges was to remember to bring the notebook as well as the homework to each class. I liked doing the homework and always remembered to bring the notebook by leaving a Post-it note on the front door of our apartment to remind me.

Spaulding was about a 30-minute taxi drive from my apartment. I was still using my Blackberry and had not even heard of Uber, so I got to Spaulding by taxi. Pam had taught me how to use a phone and a computer again as early as possible in 2012 after she explained to me what they were. I had progressed a lot from when she had tried to explain the clock to me while I was at NYU and I had been an obnoxious student. "Why 60 minutes and why 24 hours and why two hands?" She made it my responsibility to remember my appointments and my homework and to get to therapy correctly. Pam helped me get into the habit of putting every appointment into my computer and phone and checking my calendar at breakfast every day, even before I checked my e-mails. I still follow that method today and put everything, including important dates and reminders into my computer. I am often the one charged with remembering birthdays, anniversaries and other important dates for our family and friends. I had also started using Post-it notes for simple reminders around the apartment for everything—a strategy I still use every day.

I joined a book club at Spaulding that had four other rehabilitation patients. It lasted about six months and we met twice a month. The books were mostly short stories. We were not allowed to bring written notes to the sessions which was obviously an exercise in testing memory as well as other cognitive skills. It was a very good exercise for me since my memory has really been adversely affected by my injury. It was a good way for me to get out of the apartment for a few hours and get comfortable calling and taking a taxi by myself. It was also a great opportunity to meet other people and talk and debate points of view while trying to remember the thesis of the books.

Boston is a wonderful walking city and our apartment was just a few blocks walk from everything we needed. There was a Starbucks just down the street, so I would get coffee every morning and sometimes breakfast on days I didn't want to make my own. There also was a Chipotle only a few blocks away that we liked. When Pam traveled, which was now about twice a month, she knew that I would be alright on my own and could get dinner for myself. I would also occasionally walk to the boutique grocery store that was also very close to our apartment to pick up dinner for us. Whenever I did this I always stopped at St. Anthony Shrine, the Church where we went to for Mass once a month just to light a candle and say a quick prayer for my family and to thank the Lord again for my being alive and getting better.

We still never cooked. We loved to go to the North End for amazing Italian Food once a month, but our favorite Friday or Saturday night restaurant was Nebo, which we could see from our apartment. Nebo had a lot of great things on their menu, but I almost always had the Zucchini Lasagna which was a dish that beat Bobby Flay on his show. It also had al fresco seating in the warmer months which we loved. On Sunday nights we would always try to have dinner with Ian, who was only a short taxi ride away from us and have pork and vegetable dumplings from our new second favorite Chinese restaurant, "Gourmet Dumpling House." It is a tiny restaurant and the dumplings are so good that people would stand outside, even in freezing cold, for 20 minutes just to get a table. The Gourmet Dumpling House was just a short walk from our apartment, so we would order out and walk over to pick up the food. The funniest thing about the restaurant is a picture on the front wall of Michael Douglas, the famous actor, with the owner. Pam is convinced it was photo-shopped, but I'm not so sure.

It was great to see Ian and hear his stories about Medical School, which he loved but said was really challenging. Pam loved hearing about Ian's experiences since her father had been a very accomplished neurosurgeon who had, unfortunately, passed away at a very young age, when Pam was only nine. Ian had already come a long way from his "White Coat Ceremony" in the spring of 2014. Some medical schools, like Tufts, have this ceremony during a medical student's first year. It was an awesome event. Each student is given a "White Coat" symbolizing his inception into the medical field and is required to recite the Hippocratic Oath. I was so proud of Ian and so happy that I was there. Pam and I sat at a table with Peggy and Gregg. I know that Peggy was having the same feelings as me. Because he is amazing, Ian was elected to be his class President later in that year and was reelected every year he was at Tufts.

We made it through the snowiest winter in Boston history to a beautiful spring and summer. On warm sunny Saturday and Sunday mornings, we would often walk across the Boston Common to Newbury Street which had several great restaurants for brunch. Once it got warm we also wanted to play golf and found a very good public course near home, George Wright, which was in decent shape and very challenging. We really wanted to play Taconic, which was about a three-hour drive from Boston and went there as often as we could. As before, we would often play with Joan and Peter Zegras, who said I had improved a lot from the prior year. In Williamstown we would have dinner at Mezze, our favorite restaurant and during the summer have picnics on the lawn at Tanglewood. Tanglewood always has amazing classical artists performing during the summer including the Boston Pops. That summer we also got to see Sheryl Crow perform. She was awesome. I loved watching and hearing live music under the stars with a picnic dinner and the woman I loved.

I was starting to get a little better at golf, which made me very happy. I was actually shooting legitimately in the mid 90s from the white tees at Taconic, which is a difficult course. However, as I got better I also occasionally got frustrated with myself for not improving faster. Golf can be a very rewarding and a very frustrating sport in the same round. Whenever I started acting like an ass, Pam would remind me that I was dead a few years ago. This would give me the proper perspective.

CHAPTER 16

On June 16, 2015, to Neil Young's *Rockin' in the Free World*, Donald Trump came down his escalator at Trump Tower in New York and announced that he was running for President of the United States. I was on the "Trump Train" from that day. Partly because I had done business with his company and had a very good experience, but mostly because I didn't like the direction that our current President had taken the country during his almost 8 years in office. I always had an interest in politics and mostly watched CNN to get my news. I really believed that the country needed an incredibly successful businessman, not a career politician again to put the country back on the right path. And I think I was very correct. I followed the primaries, the debates and the election very carefully. I thought that Trump ran a brilliant, albeit, controversial, campaign running against 17 veteran Republican politicians and Hillary Clinton who had been anointed for President by everyone. Several brilliant and very over-paid talking heads and media "experts" had her at 90% or more chance of winning right until the evening of November 8, 2016. I had a spreadsheet of each state with their respective electoral vote tally on my table on election night and just kept highlighting the states Trump won. Everyone said he could never get to 270 electoral votes because Hillary was already starting with 86 electoral votes from California and New York. Trump won in a landslide with 304 total electoral votes. He has already done some very good things and I think he will be a great President for both his terms.

We had a great time in Boston. We really liked the Radian and really loved being able to see Ian often. Our lease was coming to an end and we had to figure out where we were going. Pam had been traveling to Phoenix almost once a month to oversee a team there and since that would likely continue, we decided that Phoenix was our favorite option. We always loved the time we spent in the Biltmore Villa. We didn't want to make the same mistake I had made in Cleveland by buying a house right away, so we agreed to rent for a year to make sure it was the right move. Our initial instinct was to look for rental apartments at the Arizona Biltmore and that area of Phoenix since we knew it so well. We didn't see anything that we loved. We told our good friend Kerry Graham that we were moving to Phoenix and asked her if she had any suggestions. She was very excited and put us in touch with a broker who suggested that we look at a gated golf community called Gainey Ranch in Scottsdale.

Gainey Ranch was awesome. After looking at a few homes in the community, we settled on a very nice 3000-square-foot, three-bedroom, two-story house, directly on the golf course at a rental price that was less than our apartment in Boston. We moved in right about the date of my birthday, October 1, 2015. To add to the serendipity of the whole affair, the owner of the house we had decided to rent had been a Board Member of Boykin Lodging Company.

Gainey Ranch is a tremendous and vast community, mostly with beautiful owned homes from two-bedroom Golf Villas to large lakeside homes. Besides golf, the community also has a great tennis facility and health club. We met with the Golf Membership Director and got a full tour of the incredible, ranch style clubhouse and the golf course. Gainey Ranch has three nine-hole championship golf courses with "Masters-style" white sand for the sand traps. We joined the Club right away. The views from the clubhouse and most of the holes are spectacular as there are surrounding mountains always in sight. An excellent perquisite to joining Gainey Ranch Golf Club is that we also became members of Club Corp. Club Corp owns and operates more than 200 private dining and golf clubs in the United States including Gainey Ranch. Since Club Corp started as a dining club, the food at Gainey Ranch is excellent and we eat at the club several days and nights every week, continuing our tradition of not cooking. To thank Kerry for introducing us to such a wonderful place, we celebrated our new-found home by treating Kerry for dinner at El Chorro at our favorite table next to the outdoor fireplace.

Kerry Graham is amazing. She was so happy that we had moved to Phoenix she offered to furnish our entire house with furniture from her large Paradise Valley home that she had put in storage when her husband Bill died. It was incredible -beautiful couches, tables, dining room and bedroom furniture, Persian rugs and outdoor furniture, including a grill. We had no idea how we were going to furnish a full nine-room house, and backyard, with furniture from our two-bedroom apartment in Boston, but Kerry took care of it for us in one dinner.

We also discussed that I wanted to continue therapy and Kerry, like the angel she is, told us that Bill had been a board member of Barrows Neurological Hospital, in Phoenix and that she would arrange to get me in to see their Rehabilitation Physicians. Barrows, like Spaulding, in Massachusetts, is the best rehabilitation center in Arizona and focuses on brain trauma. Like Spaulding in Boston, it is also where most professional athletes would go for therapy after brain injuries.

When we moved to Scottsdale, Kerry had started writing a book about her experience as a golf professional with special emphasis on the mental aspect of the game and golf teaching methodology. She was working with Ricki Linksman, who is an author and leading expert in brain-based accelerated learning techniques for all types of learners. Ricki had published the book "How to Learn Anything Quickly" in 2001. Kerry's golf teaching had always focused on the most important part of golf instruction, the mental game. Kerry asked me to edit her new book and I was thrilled and honored to do so. I was an English Major at Williams and had always been a good and very particular writer. We worked together steadily for eight months both through e-mails and in person. It was a great cognitive experience for me and I think that I helped Kerry make it a better book. Kerry's book was first published in June, 2016, but wasn't marketed for a few months due to some legal matters which I also helped Kerry with. The book title is *The Power of Mental Golf* and is a terrific read and applicable to every type of golfer who wants to improve, especially players like me. I was very proud of Kerry, and Pam and Kerry were both very proud of me for my work. I had come a long way from having to learn how to write again at NYU a few years ago.

Soon after we moved to Scottsdale, I started working weekly with Kerry on my golf game. She helped me start loving golf again and already had helped me start shooting in the 90s. Kerry had kindly given both Pam and me golf lessons as a Christmas present and about once a week for almost a year, Pam would drop me off at her office and Kerry would pick me up for a lesson. Pam's office building was adjacent to a Starbucks, so I could get coffee and breakfast before my lesson. Kerry was teaching at Papago Golf Club, considered the finest public golf course in Arizona, so we went there for our sessions. Papago is a fabulous championship course with an awesome practice range with the most spectacular mountain views. Kerry had played with me and Bill and Pam often before my injury and while she was always amazed that I could play as well as I did she never tried to fix me. She was amazed because she said I would always just line up and swing as hard as

I could, and the ball would go wherever I happened to be aiming. I had a very good short game and always putted well back then so generally I scored well. At the time of my injury I was a 4-handicap golfer for many years and almost always shot in the 70s.

Kerry, told me that she was going to make me a "golfer" not a "hitter" and she did. She has truly helped me to love the game again and always encouraged and inspired me. In our sessions, we worked on my mental approach to the game as much as the physical aspect. This was the hardest and also the most rewarding part of my golf "therapy." She also gave me the right perspective on my recovery; that this was not a sprint and I had already surpassed everyone's expectations. Everyone but me. She also was a lot tougher on me than Pam when I showed my frustration; and wasn't shy about scolding me whenever I acted like a spoiled child.

As I said, Kerry was as interested in my mental recovery and progress as my golf learning and would often send me fun and positive on-line articles that she thought might be relevant. She knew that this was the most important and challenging part of my golf recovery and I appreciated that she was not afraid to push me. She taught me how to focus on "thinking" during our sessions rather than just hitting golf balls. My favorite on-line link was to a commencement speech given by a Navy Admiral to a class of college students. I have been to many commencement speeches, some great, some abysmal, but this was one of the best. Like most commencement speeches, it was mostly about giving the students a positive and inspirational view of their future. One of the most interesting parts of the speech for me was when he talked about having to make his bed perfectly every morning before being allowed to go to breakfast. A superior soldier would be tasked with inspecting his bed every morning. He made the point that by making his bed perfectly he always started his day with an accomplishment that set a positive tone for the rest of the day.

I thought it was a great message. So, the first thing I do every morning after I kiss Pam and tell her I love her, text Riley, say my prayers and do my balance exercises is make my bed. I don't even try to do it to Navy standards, but it's funny, the Admiral was right, as simple as it sounds, I do feel better after doing it.

Pam had given me an iPhone 6 for my birthday to replace the Blackberry that I had used for many years. She told me it would be much better for me and that I would come to love it. I was skeptical at first, that skepticism lasted about two hours. The iPhone's capabilities were amazing. It was easy for Pam to teach me how to use the phone since she already had one. I had come a long way from when she tried to teach me about the clock in the hospital. She also taught me how to download and use the "apps," including Uber, so I could get to Barrows by myself, which was about 30 minutes from our house. Barrows was an amazing facility and my therapists for Physical, Speech, and Occupational were all fantastic. My physical therapist really helped me improve my balance and gave me some exercises that I still do every day. One was just standing on one leg and the other was standing with my feet vertical and touching. At the beginning I could only do each exercise for about five seconds. I got to 30 seconds with each exercise on each leg by the time my therapy ended in a year. I work on it every morning by doing both the leg lifts and the vertical feet exercises for 60 seconds on each side and now I can do the vertical feet exercise with my arms folded and my eyes closed. Pam also gave me "Perfect Pushup" paddles for my birthday. I started by doing 30 a day, now I do 60 every morning after my balance exercises.

During my sessions with my speech therapist, we focused on my speech for half the time and the other half we devoted to memory and other cognitive tests. She knew that my speech was never going to be perfect again. She would read very short stories to me and ask me questions to see how well I could remember details. We also did a lot of math exercises. I generally did better on the math tests than the memory tests. She also introduced me to the *Set Game*, a very simple looking visual perception game, that is not as simple as it seems. A perfect game is six correct answers. She also introduced me to the game *Scrabble Sprint*. I have loved to play scrabble since I was about 10 years old when I would play with my Mother. In *Scrabble Sprint* you play with seven tiles and try to make as many words as possible against a timer. *Scrabble Sprint* has the same type of bonus tiles as in the original game. When I started playing I never got a "bingo," which requires using all seven tiles to make a word. It is worth an additional 50 points. I would generally score around 350 points. Now I play both games on my computer every morning right after making coffee and breakfast and checking my calendar for the day. When I first played the *Set Game* I was lucky to get four out of six answers, now I play it until I get all six and I play *Scrabble Sprint* until I get at least 500 points, which requires at least one bingo.

With my occupational therapist I did a lot of visual, small motor and speed exercises. My favorite exercises involved a 100-foot flat screen monitor. She had several challenging exercises to choose from. When I first started it just involved a timed visual speed test involving hitting white circles that would disappear from the screen after a second. When I did well enough on that she would add a letter component to make it a bit harder. My favorite exercise however involved a rotating screen with 26 numbers and the 26 letters of the alphabet. It was a timed exercise and the challenge was to hit the numbers and letters in sequence and in alphabetical order. I was not very good at first but worked hard with my therapist until I could do it perfectly every time. Then it became a matter of improving my speed. After about a year, my therapy at Barrows ended. I think that it was a great experience and that I made a lot of progress over the last five years.

Pam and I loved being in Phoenix and loved our house. The weather is always great. I could walk to the driving range every morning which was about a five-minute walk from our house and practice for a little more than an hour and go to the health club every afternoon, which was about a 12-minute walk, and spend about 45 minutes on the elliptical machine and another 15 minutes on weight training. After working out every day in Boston and continuing that here I weigh less and am in better physical condition now than I was when Pam and I got married in 1999.

Riley was our first guest in the new house. He came for a week in early November and we had a great time playing golf almost every day. As no surprise to me with his athletic talent, Riley had become an excellent golfer and could hit his drives 300 yards, which is professional length. In my best days, when I was a 4-handicap golfer the longest I ever hit my drive was about 285 yards downhill and downwind. It was great fun playing with him and watching him play so well. He helped me a lot and I was hitting my drive an additional 10 yards when he left—of course that now made it about 220 yards. We went to our usual haunts, El Chorro and Fleming's and Kerry joined us a few times.

As was our custom, we went to Ft. Lauderdale for Thanksgiving. This year I ran the 3.2 Mile Turkey Trot at 13 minutes per mile, two minutes faster than 2015. We also had dinner with Scott and Laura who had moved into their house in Versailles in Wellington. As always, it was great to be with them. They are great friends and we have spent a lot of time together over many years. It was great fun for me to hear stories from our past adventures. Even though I don't remember those times that well, I know that we always had fun. They thought that I looked great and had made an amazing recovery.

Our next trip was to New York for Christmas. Since Le Cirque, one of the best restaurants in the world, is a member of Club Corp we were able to have a fabulous Prix Fix dinner for the cost of a bottle of wine. We had Christmas Eve at Uncle Tom's apartment where we all participated in the *Visit From St. Nicholas* reading and I will always remember that the party was the impetus for my walking.

Pam had to go Los Angeles for work in late January and I went with her. Because of work, she wasn't able to come to a dinner that I had booked for us with Riley and Billy. So, we had a boys' dinner at the City Club restaurant in LA, a Club Corp restaurant. I was able to get to and from the dinner by myself without incident. The restaurant is at the top of the City National Bank building in the financial district of LA. The views of LA, with panoramic floor to ceiling windows, and the dinner were both fantastic. It was great to see Riley and Billy. Riley seemed to be loving LA and Billy was working on several interesting projects. Billy and Riley both said that it was incredible that only a few years ago they saw me in a hospital bed with tubes coming out of every part of my body, unclear as to whether I would ever recover and walk again. Today I was not only walking, but dressed like my old self, 25 pounds lighter, and having dinner with them in a fine restaurant. To celebrate, after we finished eating, Billy ordered three shots of Jameson Irish Whiskey and we gave a toast to being together. It was and still is the only hard liquor I have had since my injury. Pam also has given up hard liquor since my injury and Paula has given up drinking alcohol completely. I know that my doctors would like me to completely give up drinking alcohol. The only time I do drink is during holidays and on special occasions, only with Pam and I only drink champagne and good wine. I did give up drinking alcoholic beer completely, except for the very occasional Guinness, which has a less alcohol content than most regular beers.

I have, however, become an aficionado in non-alcoholic (NA) beer. I now think that many NA beers taste better than regular beer. My favorite is Kaliber (by Guinness), and St. Pauli Girl, Buckler (by Heineken) and Coors are also quite very good.

For Paula and Pam's birthday in 2016, Paula, Barbara and Adam came to Scottsdale to celebrate "Birthday Week" with us. We spent time in Scottsdale and also went to Sedona and The Grand Canyon, where we hiked about seven miles a day. Walking downhill with no support still was a challenge for me but I wanted to do it, so I told the women to go ahead and I just went at my own comfortable pace. The same group went back to Cabo St. Lucas in late May, 2016 and again stayed at Adam's great home on the Sea of Cortez. We went back to Palmilla for a fantastic lunch and a round of golf. I shot in the high 80s for the first time and we had a much better time on the golf course than in 2014 and I had a better appreciation for the beauty of the course and my game. Pam and I continued our tradition of running on the beach in the morning and kayaking in the afternoon. I really wanted to go a bit faster in the Turkey Trot at Thanksgiving. Adam said that my recovery had been remarkable.

On the Friday before Father's Day in 2016 I was coming back from the gym and saw a "For Sale – Estate Sale" sign on the lawn of the house two doors down from us and, of course, I went in. The house was exactly the same layout of the house we were currently renting. There were some things about the new house that I didn't love, but it also had an amazing large brick firepit and a very large brick inground spa in the backyard which I did love. I told Pam about the house that night and she came with me the next morning to see it. She saw the same negative things as I had but also saw the same things that I really liked a lot. I knew that negotiating with an estate agent is generally easier than a normal seller agent and it was. There was the normal haggling about price, but we got the deal we wanted and on August 2, 2016, Pam closed on the house. We celebrated by going to The Boulders for the weekend. Pam still had two months left on the lease of our current house which worked out well as we were able to get all the work we wanted done in the new house without much hassle and within that time. It was also perfect because we only had to move our furniture and clothes two doors down and put them in the same spot. It was a perfect deal for us, we loved the layout of the house and the new backyard additions were awesome.

We also both loved living in Scottsdale and in the Gainey Community. I had developed a nice routine for the weekdays. I would wake up at 6:30 a.m., do my morning routine of telling Pam how much I loved her, texting Riley, saying my prayers, doing my balance exercises and pushups and making my bed. Then I would go downstairs, make coffee and breakfast which is fruit and yogurt or oatmeal, check my calendar, my e-mails and watch an episode of Perry Mason which I had loved when I was a teenager. Then I would play the *Set Game* and *Scrabble Sprint* while watching Fox News for about two hours to catch up on the news. I stopped watching CNN and MSNBC for the most part because they had stopped being credible news outlets and their coverage had become partisan, anti-Trump rhetoric ever since Trump had won the Republican Nomination. It was fun to watch all their "expert" talking heads try to explain how they had been so wrong. After a little news I would go to the driving range for about an hour and a half trying to remember what Kerry had taught me. As is often the case with golf, some days were great, some awful, but as I had learned many years ago, a bad day playing golf is still a pretty good day, especially for me. After golf it was usually a combination of news, e-mails and reading until 4:00 p.m. when I would go to the gym for about an hour and a half. The gym is about a 12-minute walk from my house and when we moved to Gainey Ranch I started by doing four miles on the elliptical machine every week day, which took about 40 minutes. Now I do the elliptical machine for five miles every day, about another 10 minutes. I always watched *The O'Reilly Factor*, which came on at 6:00 p.m. our time. I always thought that he was the best interviewer and always had the best, brightest guests. Pam usually got home around 7:00 p.m., we would have a healthy dinner that she had picked up and usually spent the evening cuddling on our couch while watching *Chopped* or *Beat Bobby Flay*. Even though we rarely cooked, we love those shows, probably because of the competition.

On Friday night if we were not going out for a more "fancy" dinner we liked to go to Morton's for Happy Hour, because they had a great bar menu and poured good wine. I could have one glass of wine. We then would catch a movie at the IPic theater which is very close by and is a great place to watch a movie. Saturday is grilling night. Usually salmon and swordfish. We would play golf on the weekends, generally as early as possible when the temperature was lowest and so we then had the whole afternoon free.

CHAPTER 17

Pam wanted to do something special for me for my 60TH birthday and she was able to put together a fantastic trip by combining a trip to London, for her work, and a trip to Ireland, for fun. We stayed at our favorite London hotel, the Marylebone. I was very comfortable by myself during the day—having breakfast in the hotel restaurant and working out during the day was easy for me. Buckingham Palace is very close to the hotel, so I could walk over to see the changing of the guard for a little tourist fun and also walk along Regent Street for a little window shopping as if I was on Fifth Avenue or Rodeo Drive. We did have one very special dinner in London, at Seven Park Place, a Michelin Star restaurant, by William Drabble. Seven Park Place is in the St. James Hotel, which is itself a 5-Star luxury hotel. We got a special table and the experience was phenomenal. The maître d' even gave us a half bottle of Sauturnes with our dessert to help celebrate my birthday.

We then went to one of our favorite places on earth, The K Club. The weather was very mild for September in Ireland and we were able to play golf all three days without getting too wet. We always ended the evening with a Guinness with Remy in the Vintage Crop Bar. On our second night there, Pam had arranged dinner for us in their signature restaurant, the River Room. Dinner was great, but Pam had told the maître d' that it was my 60TH birthday, we were loyal guests, and she wanted something special for desert. I guess the kitchen and the waiter didn't get the message and the desert came out without a candle or anything special. Pam was visibly upset and, very uncharacteristically, started crying.

The maître d' was mortified when he learned what had happened. He gave us a very nice bottle of Bollinger champagne that we had the next night with dinner in a special room, by ourselves, with Remy as our server. It all worked out, Pam had done a wonderful job, and it was a perfect birthday. We were celebrating more than my birthday, we were celebrating my comeback together.

On November 8TH, 2016 Donald Trump shocked the world and every political "expert" on the planet by becoming the President of the United States. Even more shocking is that he won in a landslide. I was very happy and now know that he will be a great President for eight years.

As usual we went to Florida for Thanksgiving with the family and I ran in the "Turkey Trot." I ran the 3.2 mile course in 13 minutes per mile, about a minute per mile faster than the past year. I was very happy and proud that my work on the treadmill for the past month had paid off. Amanda, who had also recovered amazingly since February 2012, walked the entire 5K, which was awesome.

The year 2017 started out in exciting fashion with Peter and Amanda getting married in Las Vegas. It was an intimate, mostly family affair. Pam and I stayed with Paula in an amazing suite in Mandalay Bay. On the afternoon of the rehearsal dinner Peter had arranged for all of us to have a Guinness "pint pouring" lesson in the Guinness store in the hotel. It was great fun and I suggested to Pam that we get our own Guinness pump for our house, she said "I'm sure your doctors would really like that." I was only kidding. To keep the Irish theme going, we had the rehearsal dinner at the RiRa Irish pub also in the hotel. Pam and I and the family danced the night away to an Irish band. I was very happy to be dancing after being told I would never walk again a few years ago.

The highlight of the Wedding the next day, besides the service, was the duet violin performance by Anika, Pam's niece, and

Pierrette. It was beautiful and amazing. I fully expect to see Anika performing on stage at The Met or Carnegie Hall in about 15 years.

It was a beautiful afternoon on May 21, 2016 in Boston when Ian graduated from Tufts. As President of his Class for each of his four years at Tufts, Ian gave the valedictory speech. He was awesome. I was so proud of him and just so happy to be there for the moment. He will be an incredible doctor. We had a celebratory lunch with Pam, Riley, Peggy and Gregg. I could tell that Peggy also was beaming with pride for Ian. It was also great to see Riley who said that he was really enjoying his life in LA. I gave Ian my cherished Panerai watch as a gift. I hope it brings him good fortune and that he will love it as much as I had.

Since we were in Boston we had to go to Williamstown and play golf at Taconic. We had a great time, we went to Mezze for dinner and Tunnel City for Coffee and played with our favorite Williamstown golf friends, Joan and Peter Zegras. I was shooting in the high 80s and they recalled that it wasn't that long ago that I could barely put a golf ball on a tee by myself.

Riley came to visit us in mid-June. As usual we had an awesome time and played a few days of golf. Because he is such a great athlete, even though he doesn't have the opportunity to play golf a lot he is very good at it. I humbly want to take some credit for that. One morning we were playing behind a foursome of women on the second hole of the Lakes course which is a short (310 yard) par 4. Riley teed off while the women were on the green and Riley hit such a good drive that his ball rolled onto the green while the women were putting. Even though they were never in danger the women were not happy. Riley and I drove up and apologized profusely although it was very hard for us not to laugh. I was thinking that I should go back to my old method of just swinging as hard as I could. I don't think Kerry would approve.

I was working on my golf game with Kerry through the summer. Being physically stronger and having much better balance she was able to really help me. Of course, I still needed the most work on the mental aspect of the game which is what Kerry specializes in. On September 9, I shot a 79 on the Lakes Course from the white tees. I really felt like I had reached a milestone both in my golf game and my recovery. I give tremendous credit to Kerry and have a new goal for 2018, shooting in the 70s from the championship tees.

CHAPTER 18

Bryeanna (my niece) and Matt Brzoza got married on September 16, 2017. The rehearsal dinner was on the evening before at Tim's bar, Bar Harbor. It was a beautiful night, so we were able to sit outside. I gave the following toast to Bryanna and Matt and the gathering.

> "I have been married to my beautiful and wonderful wife Pam for almost 20 years and I have some very simple advice for maintaining a happy marriage. First, say 'I Love You' to each other often, second, laugh with each other often, third, never ever go to bed angry at each other and fourth, for you Matt, learn to say, 'Yes, Dear' a lot."

The toast was well received. I had not told Pam that I was going to give the toast and she said that she was surprised when I stood up and took the microphone. I was not nervous at all and fully enjoyed doing it. Pam said that my speech was very clear, which is a testament to all my speech therapists, and that she was proud of me. I was proud of myself and look forward to my next opportunity to speak publicly.

The wedding the next day was fantastic and very special. It was held at St. John and Paul's Church in Larchmont, NY. Bryeanna was a beautiful bride and Tim gave a great toast to Bryeanna and Matt at the reception at Larchmont Yacht Club. Riley also came to the wedding which added to the fun and we danced the night away to a great band. We ended the evening on the outside porch with

Bryeanna, Matt, Tim, Siobhan, Riley, Pam and me, all having one last glass of Champagne together. It was a great day.

My brother in law, Peter, recently became the Harbor Master at the port of Honolulu, Hawaii—a well-deserved great position. Pam, Paula, Barbara and I thought we could help cheer him up by visiting him and Amanda for Thanksgiving. We had a great time. Pam and I played golf at a fabulous Club Corp course, the Royal Hawaiian, with remarkable views. The most incredible event, however, was the board surfing lesson that Peter arranged for us. Pam was very worried about me participating, afraid that I might fall and hit my head on the board and drown. I insisted on trying and reminded Pam that I still was a very strong swimmer and had done a lot of body surfing in my younger days. Our teacher was amazing. I told him about my TBI and he was especially careful with me and gave me special treatment. None of us had ever been board surfing before, but Pam, Paula and Peter were naturals. I was the worst of the group but did manage to get up three times, once riding a wave for about 15 seconds. I figure that if I could do this, I can do anything, and the experience reminded me that life is a wonderful gift that should always be embraced with passion. I truly believe that to really succeed in life you must have a personal philosophy and passion. My philosophy is simple. Continue to push myself every day to improve and to be a better husband for Pam and father for Ian and for Riley. I will continue to embrace that philosophy with great passion and am looking forward to the next challenge.

EPILOGUE

It is the day after Bryeanna's wedding and I am sitting on a deck chair next to the love of my life, Pam, at The Larchmont Yacht Club looking at the clear blue water of the Long Island Sound as I have done so many times before. At the wedding, Riley and I happened to be talking about relationships and he said something wonderful to me. He said that he hopes to have a relationship like mine and Pam's someday because the love between us is so vibrant and apparent. For myself, I didn't believe that you could love someone more every day but that is exactly how I feel with Pam every day. Her love inspired me to write this book.